Beyond Gender

Understanding Intersectional Feminism and Its Role in Social Justice

Jade Malone

The presentation of the information is without contract or any type of guarantee assurance. The trademarks that are used are without any consent, and the publication of the trademark is without permission or backing by the trademark owner. All trademarks and brands within this book are for clarifying purposes only and are the owned by the owners themselves, not affiliated with this document.

Table of Contents

Chapter 1

Introduction to Intersectional Feminism

Historical Context The Roots of Intersectionality

The roots of intersectionality trace back to a rich tapestry of social, political, and intellectual movements that sought to address the multifaceted nature of identity and oppression. Long before the term "intersectionality" was coined, the interconnected struggles of race, class, gender, and other social categories were evident in various historical contexts and movements. From the abolitionist and suffrage movements of the 19th century to the civil rights and feminist movements of the 20th century, these struggles have highlighted the need for a more inclusive and nuanced understanding of social justice.

In the mid-19th century, the abolitionist movement emerged as a powerful force against the institution of slavery in the United States. Key figures such as Sojourner Truth and Frederick Douglass recognized the intersectional nature of oppression, as they fought not only for the emancipation of enslaved people but also for the rights of women and other marginalized groups. Sojourner Truth's famous "Ain't I a Woman?" speech, delivered at the 1851 Women's Rights Convention in Akron, Ohio, eloquently captured the dual oppression faced by Black women, challenging both racial and gender-based discrimination. Her words underscored the need for a more nuanced understanding of identity and power that would later form the foundation of intersectional thought.

The suffrage movement, which sought to secure women's right to vote, also revealed the complexities of intersecting identities. While figures like Susan B. Anthony and Elizabeth Cady Stanton are often celebrated for their contributions to women's rights, the movement was not without its internal conflicts. Many suffragists prioritized the enfranchisement of white women over that of Black women and other marginalized groups, revealing a hierarchy within the movement that privileged certain identities over others. This tension would later serve as a catalyst for the development of more inclusive feminist frameworks that recognized the importance of race, class, and other social categories in the fight for gender equality.

The early 20th century witnessed the emergence of the Harlem Renaissance, a cultural and intellectual movement that celebrated Black identity and creativity. Figures like Zora Neale Hurston and Langston Hughes used their art and writing to explore the intersections of race, gender, and class, challenging dominant narratives and stereotypes. Their work laid the groundwork for later generations of thinkers and activists who would continue to interrogate the complexities of identity and power.

The mid-20th century saw the rise of the civil rights movement, which sought to dismantle systemic racism and achieve equality for African Americans. Activists like Martin Luther King Jr., Rosa Parks, and

Malcolm X played pivotal roles in advocating for racial justice, while simultaneously acknowledging the interconnected struggles of gender and class. The movement's emphasis on solidarity and collective action would later inform the development of intersectional frameworks that sought to address multiple forms of oppression.

During the same period, the feminist movement gained momentum, with figures like Betty Friedan, Gloria Steinem, and Audre Lorde pushing for women's rights and gender equality. However, the mainstream feminist movement often centered the experiences of white, middle-class women, marginalizing the voices and perspectives of women of color, working-class women, and other marginalized groups. This exclusion prompted the emergence of Black feminism, with scholars and activists like bell hooks, Angela Davis, and Kimberlé Crenshaw advocating for a more inclusive and intersectional approach to feminism.

Kimberlé Crenshaw, a legal scholar and civil rights advocate, is credited with coining the term "intersectionality" in the late 1980s. Her groundbreaking work highlighted the unique challenges faced by Black women in the legal system and beyond, illustrating how traditional frameworks of discrimination often failed to capture the complexity of their experiences. Crenshaw's scholarship drew attention to the need for an intersectional approach that recognizes the overlapping and intersecting nature of social identities and oppressions.

Crenshaw's work built upon the foundations laid by earlier thinkers and activists, drawing from the rich tradition of Black feminist thought. Writers like Audre Lorde and Patricia Hill Collins had long emphasized the importance of intersectionality in understanding the interconnected nature of race, gender, and class. Lorde's essays and poetry powerfully articulated the ways in which multiple identities intersect to shape individual experiences, while Collins's concept of the "matrix of domination" provided a framework for analyzing the complex interplay of power and oppression.

As the concept of intersectionality gained traction, it became increasingly clear that traditional feminist frameworks were insufficient in addressing the diverse experiences of women and other marginalized groups. Intersectional feminism emerged as a response to this inadequacy, advocating for a more inclusive and comprehensive understanding of gender equality that acknowledges the interconnectedness of various social categories.

The roots of intersectionality are deeply intertwined with the broader history of social justice movements. From the struggles of enslaved people and suffragists to the activism of civil rights leaders and Black feminists, the fight for equality has always been shaped by the recognition of intersecting identities and oppressions. This historical context provides a rich foundation for understanding the development of intersectional thought and its continued relevance in contemporary social justice efforts.

Today, intersectionality serves as a vital framework for analyzing and addressing the complex realities of identity and power. It challenges us to move beyond simplistic, one-dimensional understandings of oppression and to embrace a more nuanced and inclusive approach to social justice. By acknowledging the interconnected nature of race, gender, class, sexuality, ability, and other social categories, intersectional feminism offers a powerful tool for dismantling systemic inequalities and building a more just and equitable world.

Key Theorists and Foundational Works

The development of intersectional feminism has been significantly shaped by a diverse group of theorists and their foundational works. Their insights have not only illuminated the complexities of identity but also provided vital frameworks for understanding the intersections of race, gender, class, and other social categories. These theorists have each contributed unique perspectives that continue to influence contemporary feminist thought and activism.

One of the pivotal figures in the evolution of intersectional feminism is Kimberlé Crenshaw, whose work laid the groundwork for understanding how overlapping social identities create unique modes of discrimination. Her seminal essay, "Demarginalizing the Intersection of Race and Sex," introduced the term "intersectionality" and highlighted the limitations of singular approaches to addressing discrimination. By examining legal cases, Crenshaw illustrated how Black women were often marginalized within both feminist and civil rights discourses, underscoring the necessity for a more integrated analysis of oppression.

Building upon Crenshaw's work, Patricia Hill Collins further expanded the concept of intersectionality with her book, "Black Feminist Thought." This influential work explored the experiences of African American women, emphasizing the importance of recognizing how different forms of social stratification intersect to shape individual realities. Collins introduced the idea of the "matrix of domination," a framework that considers how various systems of power interact, reinforcing the need for comprehensive strategies to combat inequality. Her scholarship has been instrumental in broadening the scope of intersectional analysis to include a wider array of social categories and power dynamics.

Audre Lorde, a poet, essayist, and feminist, profoundly impacted the discourse on intersectionality through her exploration of the interconnectedness of race, gender, sexuality, and class. Her essays, such as "The Master's Tools Will Never Dismantle the Master's House," challenged the feminist movement to acknowledge and address its own internal hierarchies. Lorde's writings emphasized the importance of embracing difference and diversity as sources of strength, rather than obstacles to overcome. Her insistence on the necessity of intersectional analysis has inspired countless activists and scholars to adopt more inclusive approaches in their work.

In addition to these key figures, bell hooks has played a crucial role in advancing intersectional feminist theory. Her book, "Ain't I a Woman? Black Women and Feminism," confronts the historical exclusion of Black women from both feminist and anti-racist movements. Hooks' work underscores the importance of examining the intersections of race, gender, and class in order to fully understand the complexities of oppression. By advocating for a more inclusive feminism, she has challenged traditional narratives and broadened the scope of feminist theory to encompass a wider range of experiences and identities.

The contributions of Angela Davis, a political activist and scholar, have also been instrumental in shaping intersectional feminism. Her work on the intersections of race, gender, and class, particularly in the context of the prison-industrial complex, has provided critical insights into the systemic nature of oppression. Davis' book, "Women, Race, & Class," examines the historical development of feminist and civil rights movements, highlighting the ways in which these struggles have been interconnected. Her advocacy for prison abolition and social justice has further emphasized the need for an intersectional approach to addressing systemic inequality.

Gloria Anzaldúa, a Chicana feminist and cultural theorist, introduced the concept of "mestiza consciousness" in her groundbreaking book, "Borderlands/La Frontera: The New Mestiza." Anzaldúa's work explores the intersections of race, gender, sexuality, and cultural identity, particularly for those living in the borderlands between different cultures and worlds. Her writings emphasize the fluidity and hybridity of identity, challenging rigid binaries and advocating for a more inclusive understanding of the self. Anzaldúa's contributions have been pivotal in expanding intersectional feminism to include the experiences of Latinx and other marginalized communities.

In addition to these theorists, the Combahee River Collective, a Black feminist lesbian organization formed in the 1970s, has played a foundational role in the development of intersectional feminism. Their collective statement articulated the importance of addressing the interconnectedness of race, gender, class, and sexuality in the pursuit of social justice. The Combahee River Collective's work emphasized the significance of coalition-building and solidarity among marginalized groups, laying the groundwork for later intersectional movements and scholarship.

The foundational works of these theorists have been instrumental in shaping the discourse on intersectionality and continue to inform contemporary feminist thought and activism. Their insights have challenged traditional narratives, expanded the scope of feminist analysis, and highlighted the necessity of addressing multiple forms of oppression in the pursuit of social justice. By emphasizing the interconnectedness of social identities and power dynamics, intersectional feminism offers a comprehensive framework for understanding and addressing systemic inequality.

As we consider the contributions of these key theorists and foundational works, it becomes clear that intersectional feminism is not a static or monolithic concept. Rather, it is an evolving and dynamic framework that continues to adapt and respond to the complexities of contemporary society. By drawing upon the insights of these pioneering thinkers, we can continue to push the boundaries of feminist theory and practice, ensuring that our efforts toward social justice are as inclusive and comprehensive as possible.

Defining Intersectionality A Multidimensional Approach

Intersectionality is a transformative framework that seeks to comprehend the intricacies of identity and the multifaceted nature of oppression. It is a lens through which we can examine the overlapping and intersecting social categories that shape individual experiences and societal structures. By recognizing that race, gender, class, sexuality, ability, and other social identities do not operate in isolation, intersectionality offers a multidimensional approach to understanding the complexities of discrimination and inequality.

At its core, intersectionality challenges the notion of single-axis frameworks that view social identities as separate and distinct. Traditional approaches to feminism, for instance, often focused exclusively on gender, neglecting the ways in which race, class, and other social categories intersect with and impact gender experiences. Intersectionality, however, posits that these identities are inextricably linked, creating unique experiences of privilege and oppression that cannot be fully understood when viewed in isolation.

Consider the experiences of a Black woman navigating the workplace. Traditional feminist analysis might focus solely on her gender, while anti-racist frameworks might focus exclusively on her race. However, intersectionality recognizes that her experiences are shaped by both her race and gender, and that these aspects of her identity cannot be disentangled. She may face specific forms of discrimination that arise from the intersection of her race and gender, such as being perceived as less competent or facing stereotypes that do not apply to her white or male colleagues. By adopting an intersectional approach, we can better understand the unique challenges she faces and develop more effective strategies for addressing them.

The concept of intersectionality also extends beyond the individual level to examine the broader societal structures that perpetuate inequality. Institutions such as the legal system, healthcare, education, and the labor market are often designed in ways that privilege certain identities while marginalizing others. For example, policies that fail to account for the intersecting needs of low-income, disabled, or LGBTQ+ individuals may inadvertently reinforce existing disparities. Intersectionality calls for a critical examination of these structures, urging us to question who is included and who is excluded in the development and implementation of policies and practices.

Intersectionality also highlights the importance of recognizing privilege alongside oppression. While individuals may experience marginalization in some aspects of their identity, they may also hold privilege in others. A white woman may face gender-based discrimination, yet still benefit from racial privilege. Similarly, a wealthy Black man may encounter racism but possess economic privilege that affords him certain advantages. By acknowledging the interplay of privilege and oppression, intersectionality encourages a more nuanced understanding of social dynamics and power relations.

Furthermore, intersectionality emphasizes the significance of lived experiences and the voices of marginalized individuals in shaping our understanding of social justice. Traditional academic and policy discourses have often been dominated by those in positions of power, leading to the exclusion or misrepresentation of marginalized perspectives. Intersectional analysis values the insights and expertise of those who have firsthand experience of intersecting oppressions, recognizing that their voices are essential in developing more inclusive and equitable strategies for change.

One of the challenges of intersectionality lies in its application, particularly in contexts where resources and attention are limited. The complexity of intersectional analysis can make it difficult to address all intersecting identities simultaneously. However, this challenge also presents an opportunity for coalition-building and solidarity among diverse groups. By recognizing the interconnectedness of struggles, intersectionality fosters collaboration and mutual support among marginalized communities, allowing for the development of more comprehensive and effective approaches to social justice.

In practice, adopting an intersectional approach requires a commitment to inclusivity and reflexivity. It involves continuously questioning the assumptions and biases that underlie our understanding of identity and oppression, and actively seeking out and amplifying marginalized voices. It also necessitates a willingness to engage in difficult conversations and to confront uncomfortable truths about the ways in which privilege and power operate within our own lives and communities.

Intersectionality is not a one-size-fits-all solution, nor is it a static framework. It is a dynamic and evolving approach that requires ongoing reflection and adaptation. As new social categories and identities emerge, intersectionality offers a flexible and inclusive framework for understanding the complexities of identity and power. By embracing a multidimensional approach, we can work toward a more just and equitable society that values and respects the diverse experiences and perspectives of all individuals.

Intersectionality vs. Traditional Feminism

The evolution of feminist thought has been marked by significant shifts and developments, with intersectionality emerging as a critical framework that challenges and expands upon traditional feminism. At its inception, traditional feminism primarily focused on addressing gender inequality, advocating for women's rights and emphasizing the need for equal treatment and opportunities in a patriarchal society. While this approach laid the groundwork for significant advances in women's rights, it often failed to account for the diverse and intersecting identities that shape women's experiences. Intersectionality, by contrast, offers a more nuanced and inclusive perspective that considers the complex interplay of race, class, sexuality, ability, and other social categories alongside gender.

Traditional feminism, particularly in its early waves, was largely centered on the experiences and concerns of white, middle-class women. The suffrage movement, for example, was primarily driven by the goal of securing voting rights for women, yet it frequently sidelined the voices and needs of women of color and working-class women. This singular focus on gender, while crucial in its own right, often overlooked the ways in which race, class, and other social categories compound the challenges faced by marginalized women. As a result, many women found themselves marginalized within the feminist movement, their unique experiences and struggles rendered invisible by a narrow focus on gender alone.

Intersectionality emerged as a response to these limitations, seeking to address the gaps and exclusions present within traditional feminist frameworks. By recognizing that individuals are shaped by multiple, interconnected social identities, intersectionality provides a more comprehensive understanding of the ways in which power and oppression manifest in people's lives. This approach allows for a deeper analysis of the structural and systemic forces that perpetuate inequality, going beyond the surface-level focus on gender to consider the broader context in which individuals exist.

Consider the experiences of a Latina woman working in a male-dominated industry. Traditional feminism might focus on her gender-based challenges, such as facing sexism or the gender pay gap. However, intersectionality recognizes that her experiences are also shaped by her racial and ethnic identity, potentially exposing her to additional layers of discrimination and bias. She may encounter racial stereotypes or language barriers that compound the challenges she faces as a woman. By adopting an intersectional perspective, we can better understand the full spectrum of her experiences and develop more effective strategies for advocating for her rights and supporting her success.

One of the key distinctions between intersectionality and traditional feminism lies in their respective approaches to addressing inequality. Traditional feminism often emphasizes the need for equal treatment and opportunities, advocating for policies that promote gender equality in areas such as the workplace, education, and political representation. While these efforts are essential, they may not fully address the unique needs and challenges of marginalized groups. Intersectionality, on the other hand, calls for a more holistic approach that considers the different ways in which various forms of oppression intersect and impact individuals' lives.

Intersectionality also emphasizes the importance of centering the voices and experiences of marginalized communities within feminist discourse. Traditional feminism has often been critiqued for its tendency to prioritize the perspectives of those in positions of relative privilege, leading to the exclusion or erasure of marginalized voices. Intersectionality seeks to rectify this by advocating for the inclusion of diverse perspectives and experiences in the development of feminist theory and practice. This approach recognizes that those who are most affected by intersecting oppressions possess valuable insights and expertise that are essential for creating effective and inclusive solutions.

Furthermore, intersectionality encourages a focus on coalition-building and solidarity among diverse groups. Traditional feminism has sometimes been marked by fragmentation and division, with different factions prioritizing their own interests and goals. Intersectionality, however, emphasizes the interconnectedness of struggles and the importance of working together to achieve common objectives. By fostering collaboration and mutual support, intersectional feminism creates opportunities for building powerful coalitions that can address systemic inequality in a more comprehensive and effective manner.

Despite its numerous strengths, intersectionality is not without its challenges. Its complexity and the breadth of its scope can make it difficult to apply in practice, particularly in contexts where resources and attention are limited. However, this complexity also presents an opportunity for growth and learning, as it encourages individuals and organizations to engage in ongoing reflection and adaptation. By embracing the principles of intersectionality, we can develop more nuanced and effective approaches to addressing inequality and create a more inclusive feminist movement that values and respects the diverse experiences of all individuals.

In comparing intersectionality with traditional feminism, it is important to recognize that these frameworks are not mutually exclusive. Rather, they can complement and inform one another, providing a more comprehensive understanding of the complexities of identity and oppression. Traditional feminism has laid the foundation for many of the advances in women's rights that we enjoy today, and its focus on gender equality remains essential. However, by incorporating intersectional analysis, we can build upon this foundation and create a more inclusive and equitable feminist movement that addresses the full spectrum of social justice issues.

Relevance in Today's Society

In the tapestry of today's complex social landscape, intersectionality emerges as a vital lens through which we can examine the myriad ways identities and experiences intersect, influencing the dynamics of power, privilege, and oppression. This framework has gained considerable traction in recent years, as societies worldwide grapple with issues of inequality, discrimination, and social justice. As we navigate the intricacies of modern life, intersectionality offers a means to understand and address the systemic forces that shape our experiences and interactions.

One of the most compelling reasons for the relevance of intersectionality today is the growing recognition of diverse identities within our communities. As globalization and technological advancements bring people from different backgrounds into closer contact, the need for an inclusive approach to social justice becomes more apparent. Intersectionality allows us to acknowledge the unique ways in which race, gender, class, sexuality, ability, and other social categories interact, creating distinct experiences of privilege and marginalization. By adopting this perspective, we can better appreciate the diverse voices and stories that enrich our world, fostering empathy and understanding across cultural and social divides.

The relevance of intersectionality is also evident in the ongoing struggles for racial justice and equality. Movements such as Black Lives Matter have drawn attention to the systemic racism and violence faced by Black individuals and communities, highlighting the urgent need for intersectional analysis. By considering the intersections of race, gender, and class, we can gain a deeper understanding of the structural and institutional factors that perpetuate inequality and injustice. This approach enables us to develop more effective strategies for dismantling systemic racism and promoting equity and inclusion.

In addition to racial justice, intersectionality plays a crucial role in addressing gender inequality. While significant progress has been made in advancing women's rights, many challenges remain, particularly for marginalized groups. Women of color, LGBTQ+ individuals, disabled women, and those from low-income backgrounds often face unique barriers that are not adequately addressed by traditional feminist frameworks. Intersectionality provides a means to examine these intersecting oppressions, ensuring that our efforts to promote gender equality are inclusive and comprehensive.

The workplace is another arena where intersectionality is increasingly relevant. As organizations strive to create diverse and inclusive environments, they must recognize the ways in which intersecting identities impact employees' experiences and opportunities. Intersectionality can inform policies and practices that promote equity, such as addressing pay disparities, ensuring access to professional development and advancement, and creating supportive and inclusive workplace cultures. By adopting an intersectional approach, organizations can better support their employees and foster a more equitable and inclusive work environment.

Education is yet another critical area where intersectionality has significant implications. Schools and universities play a central role in shaping the next generation of leaders and thinkers, and it is essential that they provide inclusive and equitable learning environments. Intersectionality can inform curricula, teaching practices, and policies that promote diversity and inclusion, ensuring that all students have the opportunity to succeed. By recognizing and addressing the unique challenges faced by marginalized students, educators can create more supportive and empowering learning environments that foster academic and personal growth.

Healthcare is also an area where intersectionality is increasingly relevant. Health disparities persist across various populations, with marginalized groups often experiencing poorer health outcomes and limited access to care. Intersectionality can inform public health initiatives, policies, and practices that address these disparities, ensuring that healthcare systems are more equitable and responsive to the diverse needs of all individuals. By considering the intersections of race, gender, class, and other social categories, healthcare providers and policymakers can develop more effective strategies for promoting health equity and improving outcomes for marginalized populations.

The relevance of intersectionality extends to the realm of politics and policy-making as well. As governments and institutions grapple with complex social issues, an intersectional approach can inform more inclusive and effective policy decisions. By considering the diverse needs and experiences of marginalized communities, policymakers can develop strategies that address the root causes of inequality and promote social justice. Intersectionality can also inform advocacy efforts, empowering individuals and organizations to build coalitions and drive systemic change.

Intersectionality is a powerful tool for fostering social change and promoting equity and justice in today's society. Its relevance lies in its ability to illuminate the complex and interconnected nature of identity and oppression, providing a comprehensive framework for understanding and addressing the systemic forces that shape our world. By embracing intersectionality, we can develop more inclusive and effective approaches to social justice, ensuring that our efforts are responsive to the diverse needs and experiences of all individuals.

Chapter 2

The Intersection of Race and Gender

The Role of Race in Feminist Discourse

The role of race in feminist discourse is a profound and intricate topic that has shaped the evolution of feminist thought throughout history. To truly grasp the significance of race within this context, one must consider the origins and development of feminist movements and the ways in which race, alongside other social identities, has intersected with gender to influence the experiences and voices of women across the globe.

Historically, mainstream feminist movements have often been critiqued for their lack of inclusivity and their tendency to prioritize the concerns and experiences of white, middle-class women. This limited focus has led to the marginalization of women of color within feminist discourse, rendering their unique perspectives and struggles invisible. As a result, the voices of women who face intersecting oppressions related to both gender and race have frequently been excluded from the broader narrative.

One of the most significant contributions to feminist discourse on race came from the Black feminist movement, which emerged in response to the exclusionary practices of mainstream feminism. Black feminists, such as Angela Davis, bell hooks, and the

Combahee River Collective, have played a crucial role in highlighting the intersection of race and gender, advocating for a more inclusive and comprehensive approach to feminism. Their work has emphasized the importance of considering the unique challenges faced by women of color, who often experience discrimination and oppression along multiple axes.

For instance, the Combahee River Collective's statement articulated the interconnected nature of race, gender, and class oppression, emphasizing that the liberation of all oppressed groups is intertwined. This foundational document has been instrumental in shaping contemporary feminist thought, urging feminists to adopt an intersectional approach that values and centers the experiences of marginalized women.

The intersection of race and gender is particularly evident in the context of activism and social justice movements. Women of color have been at the forefront of numerous struggles for equality and justice, often leading movements that address both racial and gender-based oppression. Figures such as Sojourner Truth, Ida B. Wells, and Audre Lorde have left an indelible mark on feminist discourse, challenging the status quo and advocating for a more inclusive and equitable society.

In the contemporary landscape, race continues to play a pivotal role in shaping feminist discourse. The global nature of modern feminism demands an understanding of the diverse cultural, political, and economic contexts in which women live. Issues such as immigration, colonialism, and economic inequality are deeply intertwined with race and have significant implications for feminist activism and theory.

The role of race in feminist discourse is also evident in the realm of popular culture and media representation. Women of color have often been subjected to stereotypical and reductive portrayals, which perpetuate harmful narratives and reinforce systemic biases. Feminist scholars and activists have long critiqued these portrayals, advocating for more accurate and diverse representations that reflect the complexities of women's lives.

In recent years, there has been a growing recognition of the importance of amplifying the voices of women of color within feminist discourse. Social media platforms have provided new avenues for marginalized voices to be heard, enabling women of color to share their stories and experiences on a global scale. Hashtags such as #BlackLivesMatter, #SayHerName, and #MeToo have highlighted the interconnectedness of race and gender, drawing attention to the systemic injustices faced by women of color and galvanizing collective action.

Educational institutions and academic scholarship have also begun to reflect a more nuanced understanding of the role of race in feminist discourse. Courses and programs that focus on intersectional feminism and critical race theory have become increasingly prevalent, providing students with the tools to analyze and challenge the systemic structures that perpetuate inequality. This shift toward a more inclusive and intersectional approach has the potential to reshape feminist discourse, fostering a deeper understanding of the complexities of identity and oppression.

Despite these advancements, challenges remain. The feminist movement continues to grapple with issues of inclusivity and representation, and there is still much work to be done to ensure that the voices and experiences of women of color are fully integrated into feminist discourse. This requires a commitment to ongoing reflection, dialogue, and action, as well as a willingness to confront the biases and assumptions that underlie our understanding of race and gender.

Case Studies Women of Color in Feminist Movements

The power and impact of women of color in feminist movements is a testament to their resilience, leadership, and commitment to justice. Throughout history, these women have navigated the complexities of intersecting identities, confronting both gender and racial discrimination while advocating for a more inclusive and equitable society. Their stories offer valuable insights into the diverse and dynamic nature of feminist movements, highlighting the importance of centering marginalized voices in the struggle for social change.

One of the most iconic figures in the history of feminist movements is Sojourner Truth, an African American abolitionist and women's rights activist. Born into slavery in the late 18th century, Truth escaped to freedom and became a powerful speaker and advocate for the rights of African Americans and women. Her famous "Ain't I a Woman?" speech, delivered at the 1851 Women's Rights Convention in Ohio, challenged prevailing notions of race and gender, calling attention to the unique struggles faced by Black women. Truth's life and work exemplify the intersectional nature of feminist activism, as she tirelessly fought against both racial and gender oppression.

Moving into the 20th century, the contributions of women of color to feminist movements continued to grow. One notable figure is Ida B. Wells, an African American journalist, suffragist, and civil rights activist. Wells used her platform to expose the horrors of lynching in the United States, advocating for racial justice and equality. Despite facing significant opposition and threats to her life, Wells remained steadfast in her pursuit of justice, highlighting the interconnectedness of racial and gender oppression. Her work laid the groundwork for future generations of activists, emphasizing the importance of addressing systemic injustices at their roots.

The Chicana feminist movement, which emerged in the 1960s and 70s, is yet another example of the powerful influence of women of color in feminist activism. This movement sought to address the unique struggles faced by Mexican American women, who often found themselves marginalized within both the broader feminist movement and the Chicano civil rights movement. Chicana feminists such as Dolores Huerta and Gloria Anzaldúa played pivotal roles in advocating for the rights of Latinx communities, emphasizing the importance of cultural identity and intersectionality in the fight for social justice. Their work has had a lasting impact on feminist discourse, highlighting the necessity of embracing diverse perspectives and experiences.

In more recent years, the contributions of Indigenous women to feminist movements have gained increased recognition. Winona LaDuke, an Anishinaabe activist and environmentalist, has been a prominent advocate for Indigenous rights and environmental justice. Through her work with organizations such as Honor the Earth, LaDuke has emphasized the importance of protecting Indigenous lands and resources, drawing attention to the intersections of environmental and social justice. Her activism highlights the unique challenges faced by Indigenous women, who often confront both gender and cultural oppression, while advocating for the sovereignty and rights of their communities.

The rise of the Black Lives Matter movement has also underscored the critical role of women of color in contemporary feminist activism. Founded by Alicia Garza, Patrisse Cullors, and Opal Tometi, Black Lives Matter has brought global attention to the systemic racism and violence faced by Black individuals and communities. The movement's emphasis on intersectionality and inclusivity has reshaped the landscape of social justice activism, highlighting the interconnectedness of racial, gender, and economic oppression. The leadership of Black women within this movement has been instrumental in driving change and advocating for a more just and equitable society.

The #MeToo movement, founded by Tarana Burke, is another powerful example of the impact of women of color in feminist movements. Initially created to support survivors of sexual violence, particularly women of color, #MeToo has sparked a global conversation about the prevalence of sexual harassment and assault. Burke's work has emphasized the importance of centering marginalized voices in discussions about gender-based violence, advocating for a more inclusive and intersectional approach to addressing these issues. Her leadership has inspired countless individuals to come forward and share their stories, fostering a sense of solidarity and empowerment among survivors.

These case studies highlight the diverse and multifaceted contributions of women of color to feminist movements. Their activism has been instrumental in challenging traditional narratives and expanding the scope of feminist discourse to include the voices and experiences of marginalized communities. By centering the perspectives of women of color, feminist movements can become more inclusive and effective, addressing the complex and intersecting systems of oppression that shape our world.

The stories of these women also underscore the importance of coalition-building and solidarity in the fight for social justice. By working together across diverse identities and experiences, women of color have been able to amplify their voices and effect meaningful change. Their activism serves as a powerful reminder of the strength and resilience that can be found in unity, as well as the transformative potential of intersectional approaches to social justice.

Structural Racism and Gender Inequality

Structural racism and gender inequality are deeply entrenched issues that continue to shape societies across the globe, often in intricate and interwoven ways. To address these systemic problems, it is essential to understand the historical and social contexts that have allowed them to persist, as well as the mechanisms through which they operate and reinforce each other.

At the core of structural racism is a system of societal structures, policies, and practices that perpetuate racial inequity and disadvantage racial minorities. Unlike overt acts of racial discrimination, structural racism is more insidious, embedded within the very fabric of institutions such as education, healthcare, the legal system, and the labor market. This form of racism is often invisible to those not directly affected by it, yet it consistently produces and perpetuates disparities in outcomes across racial groups.

Similarly, gender inequality is sustained by a collection of societal norms, attitudes, and institutional practices that privilege men over women and other gender minorities. This inequality manifests in various ways, including disparities in income and employment opportunities, unequal access to education and healthcare, and the prevalence of gender-based violence. Like structural racism, gender inequality is maintained by systems that normalize and perpetuate unequal power relations between genders.

The intersection of structural racism and gender inequality creates compounded challenges for individuals who belong to multiple marginalized groups. Women of color, for instance, often face unique barriers that cannot be fully understood through the lens of either racism or sexism alone. These barriers are the result of intersecting systems of oppression that amplify the effects of both structural racism and gender inequality, creating distinct experiences of disadvantage.

In the educational system, structural racism and gender inequality can manifest through disparities in access to quality education and resources. Schools in predominantly minority and low-income communities often receive less funding, leading to larger class sizes, fewer extracurricular opportunities, and outdated educational materials. This lack of resources disproportionately affects girls of color, who may face additional challenges related to cultural biases and stereotypes. These educational disparities can have long-lasting effects, limiting opportunities for higher education and career advancement.

The labor market is another area where structural racism and gender inequality intersect to create disparities in employment opportunities and wages. Women of color often face a double disadvantage in the workplace, experiencing both racial and gender discrimination. This can result in lower wages, fewer opportunities for career advancement, and greater job insecurity compared to their white and male counterparts. The wage gap is particularly pronounced for women of color, who earn significantly less than both white women and men of all races. Addressing these disparities requires targeted policies that consider the intersecting impacts of race and gender on economic outcomes.

Healthcare is yet another domain where structural racism and gender inequality intersect to produce unequal outcomes. Women of color are more likely to experience barriers to accessing quality healthcare, including lack of insurance, limited availability of culturally competent care, and biases within the healthcare system. These barriers can contribute to disparities in health outcomes, such as higher rates of maternal mortality and chronic health conditions among women of color. To address these inequities, it is crucial to implement policies that promote equitable access to healthcare and address the social determinants of health that disproportionately affect marginalized communities.

The criminal justice system also reflects the intersection of structural racism and gender inequality. Women of color are disproportionately affected by mass incarceration and policing practices that target minority communities. These practices not only perpetuate racial disparities in incarceration rates but also have significant social and economic consequences for families and communities. Women who have been incarcerated often face additional challenges upon reentry, including discrimination in employment and housing, which can exacerbate the cycle of poverty and marginalization.

Addressing the intersection of structural racism and gender inequality requires a multifaceted approach that includes policy reform, community engagement, and education. Policymakers must prioritize equity and inclusion in all areas of legislation, ensuring that the needs and experiences of marginalized communities are considered in the development and implementation of policies. This includes investing in education and healthcare, promoting fair labor practices, and reforming the criminal justice system to eliminate discriminatory practices.

Community engagement is also essential in addressing these systemic issues. Grassroots organizations and activists play a crucial role in advocating for change and holding institutions accountable for their practices. By amplifying the voices of those most affected by structural racism and gender inequality, these organizations can drive meaningful change and promote a more equitable society.

Education is another critical component of addressing structural racism and gender inequality. By raising awareness of these issues and their interconnected nature, we can foster greater understanding and empathy across diverse communities. Educational initiatives should aim to challenge stereotypes and biases, promote critical thinking, and encourage individuals to recognize and address their own privileges and biases.

Cultural Representation and Stereotypes

Cultural representation and stereotypes wield immense power in shaping perceptions, attitudes, and societal norms. They influence how individuals see themselves and others, playing a significant role in perpetuating or dismantling systemic inequalities. Understanding the impact of cultural representation and stereotypes is crucial in the pursuit of a more inclusive and equitable society.

Cultural representation refers to the ways in which diverse identities, experiences, and communities are depicted in media, literature, art, and other cultural forms. Accurate and inclusive representation can foster understanding, empathy, and respect among diverse groups. However, when representation is limited or distorted, it can reinforce harmful stereotypes and perpetuate discrimination.

Stereotypes are oversimplified and generalized beliefs about a particular group of people. They often arise from a lack of understanding or exposure to diverse perspectives and can lead to prejudice and bias. Stereotypes reduce individuals to a set of characteristics that may not accurately reflect their experiences or identities, ignoring the complexity and diversity within any group.

In the realm of media, cultural representation and stereotypes wield considerable influence. Films, television shows, and advertisements often serve as primary sources of information about different cultures and identities. When media representations are narrow or rely on stereotypes, they can shape public perceptions and reinforce existing biases.

Consider the portrayal of women in media. Historically, women have often been depicted in limited roles, such as the nurturing mother, the seductive femme fatale, or the helpless damsel in distress. These portrayals perpetuate stereotypes about women's capabilities, reinforcing traditional gender roles and limiting the perception of women's potential and agency. Such representations can have real-world consequences, influencing how women are treated in society and the opportunities available to them.

Similarly, racial and ethnic stereotypes are pervasive in media representations. Characters from minority backgrounds are often portrayed in stereotypical roles, such as the "angry Black woman," the "submissive Asian," or the "fiery Latina." These portrayals reduce complex identities to simplistic caricatures, perpetuating harmful stereotypes and contributing to the marginalization of minority communities. The consequences of such representation extend beyond the screen, affecting how individuals from these communities are perceived and treated in everyday life.

The impact of cultural representation and stereotypes is not limited to gender and race. LGBTQ+ individuals, people with disabilities, and other marginalized groups are also affected by limited and stereotypical portrayals. When media fails to accurately represent the diversity within these communities, it can contribute to misunderstanding, discrimination, and exclusion.

Addressing the issue of cultural representation and stereotypes requires a multifaceted approach that involves creators, consumers, and policymakers. Content creators have a responsibility to ensure that their work reflects the diversity and complexity of the world we live in. This includes actively seeking out and amplifying voices from marginalized communities, challenging stereotypes, and portraying characters and stories with depth and authenticity.

Consumers also play a critical role in shaping cultural representation. By actively seeking out and supporting diverse media, consumers can signal to creators and producers that there is a demand for inclusive and accurate representation. Engaging critically with media, questioning stereotypes, and advocating for more diverse content can help drive change in how cultural representation is approached.

Policymakers and industry leaders can influence cultural representation by implementing policies and practices that promote diversity and inclusion in media and entertainment. This may include supporting initiatives that provide opportunities for underrepresented creators, establishing guidelines to prevent harmful stereotypes, and ensuring that media organizations are held accountable for their portrayals of diverse communities.

Education is another powerful tool in challenging stereotypes and promoting inclusive representation. By incorporating diverse perspectives into curricula and encouraging critical thinking, educators can help students recognize and question stereotypes, fostering a more nuanced understanding of different cultures and identities. This approach can empower individuals to challenge bias and advocate for more inclusive representation in all areas of society.

The impact of cultural representation and stereotypes also extends to the workplace. Organizations that prioritize diversity and inclusion in their branding, advertising, and internal communications can create more inclusive environments and foster a sense of belonging among employees and customers. By challenging stereotypes and promoting diverse representation, businesses can enhance their reputation, attract a broader customer base, and contribute to positive social change.

Ultimately, the journey toward more accurate and inclusive cultural representation requires collective effort and commitment. By challenging stereotypes, amplifying diverse voices, and advocating for representation that reflects the richness and complexity of human experience, we can work towards a society that values and respects all individuals. This endeavor not only benefits marginalized communities but enriches society as a whole, fostering understanding, empathy, and connection across diverse cultures and identities.

Activism and Advocacy Voices from the Margins

Activism and advocacy have long been the driving forces behind social change, championing the rights of marginalized communities and challenging entrenched systems of power. The voices from the margins—those often overlooked or silenced—hold immense power in shaping the trajectory of movements for justice and equality. These voices, rich with diverse experiences and perspectives, have contributed to the dynamic and transformative nature of activism throughout history.

To understand the power of marginalized voices in activism, one must first recognize the unique challenges and barriers these individuals face. Often, marginalized communities confront multiple layers of discrimination and oppression, whether based on race, gender, sexuality, ability, or socioeconomic status. This intersection of identities means that mainstream narratives frequently fail to capture the full complexity of their experiences. Yet, it is precisely this complexity that equips individuals from the margins with a nuanced understanding of injustice, enabling them to articulate and advocate for solutions that address the root causes of systemic inequality.

One of the most striking examples of activism from the margins is the role of Indigenous communities in environmental justice movements. Indigenous activists have been at the forefront of efforts to protect land, water, and natural resources, drawing attention to the profound impact of climate change and environmental degradation on their communities. Their advocacy is deeply rooted in a holistic understanding of the interconnectedness of people and the environment, challenging dominant narratives that prioritize economic gain over ecological sustainability. By centering Indigenous knowledge and leadership, these movements have redefined the conversation around environmental justice, highlighting the importance of sustainable and inclusive practices.

Similarly, LGBTQ+ activists from marginalized backgrounds have been instrumental in advancing the rights of sexual and gender minorities. Historically, transgender women of color, such as Marsha P.

Johnson and Sylvia Rivera, played pivotal roles in the early LGBTQ+ rights movement, challenging both societal norms and exclusionary practices within the movement itself. Their advocacy has helped to broaden the scope of LGBTQ+ activism, emphasizing the need for an intersectional approach that considers the unique experiences of individuals at the intersection of multiple forms of oppression.

In the realm of racial justice, the Black Lives Matter movement stands as a powerful testament to the impact of marginalized voices in activism. Founded by Black women in response to systemic racism and police violence, the movement has galvanized individuals and communities worldwide to demand accountability and reform. By centering the experiences of Black individuals and communities, Black Lives Matter has shifted the national and global discourse on race, highlighting the pervasive nature of structural racism and the urgent need for systemic change.

Activists from the margins have also been at the forefront of movements for gender equality, advocating for the rights of women and gender minorities across the globe. Malala Yousafzai, a Pakistani activist and Nobel laureate, has become a symbol of the fight for girls' education, using her platform to advocate for the rights of young women to access education and opportunities. Her activism, grounded in her own experiences of marginalization and resistance, has inspired countless individuals to join the fight for gender equality and empowerment.

The power of activism and advocacy from the margins lies not only in the ability to challenge and transform existing systems but also in the creation of spaces for solidarity and community-building. Marginalized activists often emphasize the importance of collective action and mutual support, recognizing that the struggle for justice is interconnected and requires the collaboration of diverse communities. This emphasis on solidarity fosters a sense of belonging and empowerment, enabling individuals from the margins to build networks of support and amplify their voices.

To support and amplify the voices of marginalized activists, it is crucial to create inclusive and equitable spaces within movements and organizations. This involves actively challenging exclusionary practices and biases, ensuring that leadership and decision-making reflect the diversity of the communities being served. It also requires a commitment to listening to and valuing the perspectives and experiences of marginalized individuals, recognizing their expertise and leadership in the fight for justice.

Education and awareness-raising are also essential components of supporting activism from the margins. By providing platforms for marginalized voices to share their stories and insights, educational institutions, media outlets, and community organizations can help to challenge stereotypes and misconceptions, fostering greater understanding and empathy. This process of education and awareness-raising can also empower individuals from marginalized backgrounds to advocate for themselves and their communities, equipping them with the tools and knowledge needed to effect change.

Moreover, allyship plays a critical role in supporting marginalized activists. Allies can use their privilege and influence to amplify the voices of marginalized individuals, advocating for policies and practices that promote equity and inclusion. This involves recognizing and addressing one's own biases and privileges, as well as actively working to dismantle the systems of oppression that perpetuate inequality. True allyship requires a commitment to ongoing learning, reflection, and action, recognizing that the struggle for justice is a collective and continuous effort.

Chapter 3

Class, Socioeconomics, and Feminist Theory

Economic Disparities and Feminist Perspectives

Economic disparities have long been a focal point in feminist discourse, as financial independence and access to resources are crucial for empowering women and achieving gender equality. Feminist perspectives on economic inequality highlight the systemic barriers that disproportionately affect women, particularly those from marginalized communities, and offer insights into how these challenges can be addressed through policy reform, advocacy, and community action.

One of the most significant economic disparities affecting women is the gender pay gap, which refers to the difference in earnings between men and women. This gap persists across various sectors and industries, with women typically earning less than their male counterparts for the same work. Factors contributing to the pay gap include discrimination, occupational segregation, and differences in work experience and education. However, these explanations often fail to account for the systemic nature of the issue, which is rooted in deeply ingrained societal norms and structures that devalue women's work and contributions.

Feminist perspectives emphasize the importance of addressing the root causes of the gender pay gap, rather than simply focusing on surface-level solutions. This involves challenging traditional gender roles and expectations, advocating for policies that promote pay transparency and equity, and encouraging the participation of women in higher-paying, male-dominated fields. Additionally, addressing the pay gap requires a reevaluation of the value placed on work typically performed by women, such as caregiving and domestic labor, which is often undervalued and undercompensated.

Beyond the pay gap, economic disparities also manifest in the form of unequal access to resources and opportunities. Women, particularly those from marginalized communities, often face barriers to obtaining education, healthcare, and financial services, which can limit their ability to achieve economic independence and stability. These barriers are exacerbated by systemic discrimination and bias, which can restrict women's access to credit, capital, and property ownership.

To address these disparities, feminist perspectives advocate for policies and initiatives that promote equal access to resources and opportunities for all individuals, regardless of gender or background. This includes supporting programs that provide affordable childcare and parental leave, which can enable women to participate more fully in the workforce. It also involves promoting access to education and training programs that equip women with the skills and knowledge needed to succeed in a rapidly changing economy.

Feminist perspectives also highlight the importance of intersectionality in understanding and addressing economic disparities. Women of color, LGBTQ+ individuals, and women with disabilities often face compounded challenges that cannot be fully addressed through a one-size-fits-all approach. Intersectional feminism calls for a nuanced understanding of how different identities intersect to shape individuals' experiences of economic inequality, and advocates for targeted policies and initiatives that address these unique challenges.

One area where intersectionality is particularly relevant is in the context of the informal economy, where many women, especially those from marginalized communities, find themselves working. Informal work, which includes jobs that are not regulated or protected by labor laws, often lacks the stability, benefits, and protections associated with formal employment. Women engaged in informal work may face exploitation, unsafe working conditions, and limited access to social protection programs, all of which contribute to economic insecurity.

Addressing the challenges faced by women in the informal economy requires a multifaceted approach that includes extending labor protections and social benefits to informal workers, promoting fair wages and working conditions, and supporting the transition to formal employment where possible. Additionally, it involves recognizing and valuing the contributions of informal workers to the economy, and advocating for policies that enhance their economic security and wellbeing.

In addition to policy reform and advocacy, community action plays a vital role in addressing economic disparities and promoting gender equality. Grassroots organizations and initiatives can empower women to take control of their economic futures by providing resources, support, and opportunities for skill-building and entrepreneurship. Community-based programs that focus on financial literacy, cooperative enterprises, and collective bargaining can help women build economic resilience and challenge the systems that perpetuate inequality.

Feminist perspectives also underscore the importance of global solidarity in addressing economic disparities, particularly in the context of globalization and neoliberal economic policies. These policies have often exacerbated economic inequalities, disproportionately affecting women in developing countries who are engaged in low-wage, labor-intensive industries. Feminist activism on a global scale calls for fair trade practices, ethical sourcing, and corporate accountability to ensure that the benefits of globalization are shared equitably and do not come at the expense of marginalized communities.

Ultimately, achieving economic equality requires a comprehensive and collaborative effort that involves policymakers, businesses, communities, and individuals. Feminist perspectives provide valuable insights into the systemic nature of economic disparities and offer a framework for understanding and addressing these challenges in a way that promotes justice and equity for all. By centering the voices and experiences of marginalized individuals and advocating for policies that prioritize equity and inclusion, we can work towards a more just and equitable economic system that empowers all individuals to thrive.

The Impact of Class on Gender Equality

Class plays a profound role in shaping the landscape of gender equality, often creating compounding challenges that are difficult to disentangle. The intersection of class and gender reveals a complex tapestry of power dynamics and access to resources, which can either facilitate or hinder progress toward equality. Understanding the nuanced impact of class on gender equality requires us to examine the ways in which economic status influences opportunities, agency, and the lived experiences of individuals.

Class impacts access to education, a critical factor in achieving gender equality. While education is widely recognized as a pathway to empowerment, socioeconomic status can significantly limit or expand educational opportunities, particularly for women and girls. In low-income families, girls may face pressure to prioritize domestic responsibilities over schooling, or they may be pulled out of school entirely to contribute to family income. This dynamic perpetuates a cycle of poverty and limited opportunity, as education is often a stepping stone to better employment prospects and economic independence.

In contrast, individuals from higher socioeconomic backgrounds generally have greater access to quality education and resources, which can facilitate higher academic achievement and career advancement. This disparity underscores the importance of addressing class-based barriers to education, such as providing scholarships, supporting community-based educational initiatives, and advocating for policy changes that promote equal access to quality education for all, regardless of economic status.

The labor market further illustrates the intersection of class and gender. Women from lower-income backgrounds are more likely to be employed in low-wage, unstable jobs with limited benefits and protections. These positions often lack upward mobility and expose women to exploitative working conditions, reinforcing economic insecurity. Moreover, women in low-income jobs often face the double burden of paid labor and unpaid domestic work, as they are expected to manage household responsibilities alongside their employment.

Conversely, women from higher-income backgrounds may have access to more lucrative and stable employment opportunities, often accompanied by benefits such as paid leave and healthcare. These advantages can provide greater economic security and flexibility, enabling women to pursue career advancement and balance work and family life more effectively. However, even in higher-paying sectors, women may encounter gender biases and barriers to leadership positions, highlighting the persistence of gender inequality across all class levels.

Class also influences access to healthcare, which is intrinsically linked to gender equality. Women from lower socioeconomic backgrounds are more likely to face barriers to accessing healthcare services, including reproductive health services, due to cost, lack of insurance, and limited availability of providers. This can result in poorer health outcomes and reduced autonomy over reproductive choices, further entrenching economic and gender disparities.

Addressing healthcare disparities requires a commitment to expanding access to affordable and comprehensive healthcare for all individuals, regardless of class. This includes advocating for policies that ensure reproductive rights and services are accessible and affordable, as well as supporting community health initiatives that provide culturally competent care to underserved populations.

The impact of class on gender equality extends to social and political participation. Economic resources often correlate with political influence and the ability to advocate for change. Women from affluent backgrounds may have greater access to networks, platforms, and resources that enable them to participate in political processes and advocate for policies that promote gender equality. In contrast, women from lower-income backgrounds may face barriers to political participation, such as lack of time, financial constraints, and limited access to information and networks.

To promote equitable political participation, it is essential to create inclusive spaces and opportunities for women from diverse class backgrounds to engage in political processes. This can include supporting grassroots organizations, providing training and resources for women interested in political leadership, and advocating for policies that reduce barriers to political participation, such as campaign finance reform and accessible voting procedures.

The intersection of class and gender also shapes cultural norms and expectations, influencing how gender roles are perceived and enacted across different socioeconomic contexts. In some communities, traditional gender roles may be more rigidly enforced, limiting women's opportunities for education and employment. In others, economic necessity may drive a more egalitarian approach to gender roles, as both partners contribute to household income and decision-making.

Challenging and redefining cultural norms requires a collective effort that involves community engagement, education, and advocacy. By promoting narratives that celebrate diverse expressions of gender and empower individuals to challenge traditional roles, we can contribute to a more inclusive and equitable society that values the contributions of all individuals, regardless of class or gender.

Ultimately, achieving gender equality requires an intersectional approach that acknowledges the impact of class on individuals' experiences and opportunities. By addressing the systemic barriers created by class and gender, we can work towards a more equitable society where all individuals have the opportunity to thrive. This involves advocating for policies and initiatives that promote economic security, access to education and healthcare, and equitable political participation, as well as challenging cultural norms that perpetuate inequality.

Labor Rights and Feminist Economics

In the quest for gender equality, labor rights and feminist economics emerge as pivotal areas of focus. Understanding the intersection of these fields reveals the critical role that fair labor practices and economic policies play in empowering women and fostering equitable societies. Feminist economics, in particular, challenges traditional economic theories by highlighting the unique contributions and experiences of women in the workforce, advocating for policies that address gender disparities and elevate the value of unpaid labor.

Labor rights form the foundation of an equitable workforce, ensuring that all individuals have access to fair wages, safe working conditions, and the freedom to organize and advocate for their rights. Historically, the labor movement has been instrumental in securing essential protections for workers, yet women have often been marginalized within these movements, their specific needs and contributions overlooked. Feminist economists emphasize the importance of centering women's voices and experiences in discussions about labor rights, recognizing that gender-specific barriers continue to hinder women's full participation in the workforce.

A key issue in labor rights is the persistent gender pay gap, where women earn less than men for comparable work. This disparity is not merely a reflection of individual choices but is deeply rooted in systemic discrimination and occupational segregation. Women are often concentrated in lower-paying industries and positions, a phenomenon known as "occupational crowding," which limits their economic mobility and access to higher-paying roles. Feminist economics advocates for policies that promote pay equity, such as transparency in compensation, support for women in leadership, and initiatives that encourage the entry of women into male-dominated fields.

Another critical aspect of labor rights is the recognition and valuation of unpaid labor, predominantly performed by women. Traditional economic models often ignore the contributions of unpaid work, such as caregiving and domestic responsibilities, which are essential to the functioning of economies and societies. This oversight not only undervalues women's labor but also perpetuates gender inequalities by reinforcing the notion that unpaid work is less valuable. Feminist economists call for the inclusion of unpaid labor in economic analyses and policy-making, advocating for measures such as paid family leave, affordable childcare, and the redistribution of domestic responsibilities to promote gender equity.

The informal economy is another area where labor rights and feminist economics intersect. Women, particularly those from marginalized communities, are disproportionately represented in informal work, which often lacks legal protections, benefits, and job security. This precarious employment can expose women to exploitation, unsafe working conditions, and economic instability. Addressing the challenges of the informal economy requires extending labor protections to informal workers, promoting fair wages and working conditions, and supporting pathways to formal employment. Feminist economics emphasizes the importance of recognizing and valuing the contributions of informal workers, advocating for policies that enhance their economic security and wellbeing.

Feminist economics also challenges traditional notions of productivity and efficiency, advocating for a more holistic understanding of economic value that encompasses social and environmental factors. This perspective calls for a reevaluation of economic policies and practices that prioritize profit over people and the planet, emphasizing the need for sustainable and inclusive growth. By integrating feminist principles into economic analyses and decision-making, policymakers can develop strategies that address the root causes of gender inequality and promote a more just and equitable economy for all.

A critical component of advancing labor rights and feminist economics is education and awareness-raising. By fostering a deeper understanding of the systemic barriers that perpetuate gender disparities in the workforce, individuals and organizations can become more effective advocates for change. Educational initiatives should aim to challenge stereotypes and biases, promote critical thinking, and encourage individuals to recognize and address their own privileges and biases.

Collaboration and solidarity are also essential in advancing labor rights and feminist economics. By building alliances across diverse communities and movements, individuals and organizations can amplify their voices and advocate for policies that promote equity and inclusion. This collective action can drive meaningful change in labor practices and economic policies, creating a more equitable and inclusive society for all.

Policymakers, employers, and labor organizations play a crucial role in advancing labor rights and feminist economics. By implementing policies and practices that promote gender equity, such as equal pay initiatives, family-friendly workplace policies, and support for women in leadership, these stakeholders can contribute to a more inclusive and equitable workforce. Additionally, labor organizations can prioritize the needs and voices of women workers, advocating for their rights and ensuring that their contributions are valued and recognized.

Access to Education and Resources

Access to education and resources is a cornerstone of empowerment, offering individuals the opportunity to transcend socio-economic barriers and realize their potential. For women and marginalized communities, this access is not just a personal benefit but a catalyst for broader societal change. The impact of education extends far beyond the classroom, influencing economic stability, health outcomes, and civic participation. Understanding the intricacies of access to education and resources illuminates the path to equity and inclusion.

Education serves as a powerful tool for social mobility, yet disparities in access persist, influenced by factors such as geography, gender, and socio-economic status. In many regions, girls face significant barriers to education, ranging from cultural norms that prioritize boys' education to logistical challenges like inadequate transportation and unsafe school environments. These obstacles often lead to higher dropout rates among girls, limiting their future opportunities and perpetuating cycles of poverty.

Addressing these barriers requires a multifaceted approach. Infrastructure improvements, such as building safe and accessible schools, can alleviate logistical challenges. Community engagement programs that promote the value of girls' education can shift cultural perceptions and encourage families to prioritize schooling for their daughters. Additionally, scholarship programs and financial incentives can ease the economic burdens that often prevent girls from attending school.

Beyond primary education, access to higher education and vocational training is crucial for economic empowerment. Women and marginalized communities frequently encounter obstacles in pursuing advanced education, including financial constraints and limited availability of programs that cater to their specific needs. Expanding access to scholarships, grants, and affordable educational institutions can mitigate these challenges, enabling more individuals to pursue higher education and specialized training.

Vocational training programs tailored to local economic needs can also play a vital role in empowerment. By equipping individuals with practical skills and knowledge, these programs can enhance employability and provide pathways to economic independence. Partnerships between educational institutions, businesses, and government agencies can ensure that vocational training aligns with labor market demands, creating a mutually beneficial ecosystem that supports both individuals and the economy.

Access to resources is another critical aspect of empowerment, encompassing everything from healthcare and financial services to technology and information. For many marginalized communities, systemic barriers limit access to these essential resources, compounding existing inequalities. Addressing these disparities requires targeted interventions that prioritize inclusivity and equity.

Healthcare access, for instance, is a fundamental right that significantly impacts quality of life and economic stability. Women, particularly those in rural or underserved areas, often face challenges in accessing comprehensive healthcare services, including reproductive health and maternal care. Expanding healthcare infrastructure, training community health workers, and implementing mobile health services can bridge these gaps, ensuring that all individuals have access to the care they need.

Financial inclusion is another crucial element of resource access. Women and marginalized communities frequently encounter obstacles in obtaining financial services, such as banking, credit, and insurance. These barriers can restrict economic opportunities and perpetuate financial insecurity. Promoting financial literacy, expanding access to microfinance, and supporting women-owned businesses can enhance financial inclusion, empowering individuals to take control of their economic futures.

Technology and information access are increasingly important in today's digital age, influencing everything from education and employment to communication and advocacy. Yet, the digital divide remains a significant barrier, with marginalized communities often lacking access to the technology and skills needed to thrive in a digital world. Expanding internet connectivity, providing affordable devices, and offering digital literacy programs can help bridge this divide, ensuring that all individuals have the opportunity to participate in and benefit from the digital economy.

The role of policy and advocacy in enhancing access to education and resources cannot be overstated. Governments and organizations must prioritize policies that promote equity and inclusion, addressing systemic barriers and investing in programs that support marginalized communities. This includes implementing quotas or affirmative action programs to ensure diverse representation in educational institutions and workplaces, as well as advocating for policies that protect and promote the rights of women and marginalized groups.

Community-based initiatives and grassroots organizations also play a vital role in enhancing access to education and resources. By working directly with communities, these organizations can identify specific needs and tailor programs to address them effectively. Community engagement, empowerment, and capacity-building are key components of successful initiatives, fostering a sense of ownership and agency among participants.

Collaboration and partnerships are essential in advancing access to education and resources. By working together, governments, non-governmental organizations, businesses, and communities can leverage their unique strengths and resources to create sustainable and impactful solutions. These partnerships can facilitate the sharing of knowledge, expertise, and resources, enhancing the effectiveness and reach of initiatives.

As we navigate the complexities of access to education and resources, it is essential to adopt an intersectional approach that recognizes the diverse identities and experiences of individuals. By understanding and addressing the unique challenges faced by different communities, we can develop more inclusive and effective strategies that promote equity and empowerment for all.

Class Struggle and Feminist Solidarity

Class struggle and feminist solidarity converge in a powerful alliance that seeks to dismantle the oppressive structures of both capitalism and patriarchy. This partnership is not just strategic; it is essential for achieving a more equitable and just society. By understanding the interplay between class and gender, we can better equip ourselves to address the systemic inequalities that affect individuals across different spectrums of society.

The roots of class struggle lie in the economic disparities and power imbalances inherent in capitalist systems. These disparities manifest in various ways, from income inequality and job insecurity to limited access to essential resources like healthcare and education. For women, these challenges are often compounded by gender-based discrimination, creating layered obstacles that impede progress toward equality.

Feminist solidarity in the context of class struggle involves recognizing these intersecting oppressions and working collaboratively to address them. It requires an understanding that the fight for gender equality cannot be separated from the fight for economic justice. Women, particularly those from marginalized and working-class backgrounds, often bear the brunt of economic inequalities, making it imperative that feminist movements incorporate class analysis into their advocacy.

One of the key areas where class struggle and feminist solidarity intersect is in the labor market. Women, especially those in low-income brackets, frequently occupy precarious and undervalued positions. These roles are characterized by low wages, limited benefits, and a lack of job security. The gig economy, for instance, has grown as a sector where many women find employment, yet it often lacks the protections and stability of traditional jobs. To address these issues, feminist solidarity must include advocating for labor rights that ensure fair wages, benefits, and working conditions for all workers, regardless of gender or class.

Moreover, feminist solidarity entails challenging the devaluation of work traditionally performed by women, such as caregiving and domestic labor. These roles, often unpaid or underpaid, are crucial to the functioning of society and the economy. By advocating for policies that recognize and compensate this labor, such as paid family leave and childcare support, feminist movements can help to elevate the economic status of women across class lines.

Housing is another domain where class struggle and feminist solidarity intersect. The affordability crisis in urban areas disproportionately affects women, particularly single mothers and women of color, who are more likely to experience housing instability and homelessness. Feminist solidarity in this context means advocating for affordable housing policies and tenant protections that prioritize the needs of vulnerable populations. It also involves supporting community-led housing initiatives that empower residents to take control of their living situations.

Healthcare access is similarly impacted by class and gender. Women, especially those from low-income backgrounds, often face barriers to accessing comprehensive healthcare services, including reproductive health care. Feminist solidarity calls for a healthcare system that is equitable and accessible to all, regardless of economic status. This includes advocating for universal healthcare policies and supporting community health programs that provide affordable care to underserved populations.

Education is a powerful tool for overcoming class and gender barriers, yet access to quality education remains unequal. Women from lower socio-economic backgrounds may face financial constraints, limiting their ability to pursue higher education and career advancement. Feminist solidarity involves supporting initiatives that provide scholarships, mentorship, and resources to women from underprivileged backgrounds, enabling them to access and succeed in educational opportunities.

Feminist solidarity in class struggle also means amplifying the voices of marginalized women who are often excluded from mainstream movements. Women of color, immigrants, and LGBTQ+ individuals bring vital perspectives and experiences to the table, and their leadership is essential for building an inclusive and effective movement. By centering these voices, feminist movements can better address the diverse needs and challenges faced by different communities.

Activism and advocacy are at the heart of feminist solidarity in class struggle. Grassroots movements and community organizations play a vital role in mobilizing individuals and effecting change. These groups often work at the intersection of class and gender, addressing issues such as wage theft, workplace discrimination, and access to social services. By supporting and collaborating with these organizations, individuals can contribute to a broader movement for justice and equality.

Collaboration across movements is key to advancing class struggle and feminist solidarity. By building alliances with labor unions, social justice organizations, and other advocacy groups, feminist movements can strengthen their impact and reach. These partnerships allow for the sharing of resources, knowledge, and strategies, enhancing the effectiveness of collective action.

Policy advocacy is another crucial component of feminist solidarity in class struggle. By engaging with policymakers and advocating for legislation that addresses the root causes of economic and gender inequality, feminist movements can drive systemic change. This includes pushing for policies that promote pay equity, workers' rights, affordable housing, and accessible healthcare and education.

Education and awareness-raising are essential for fostering feminist solidarity in class struggle. By educating individuals about the intersection of class and gender, feminist movements can build a more informed and engaged base of supporters. This includes challenging stereotypes and biases, promoting critical thinking, and encouraging individuals to recognize and address their own privileges and biases.

Chapter 4

LGBTQ+ Rights and Feminism

The Interplay Between Gender Identity and Feminism

Gender identity and feminism are intricately connected, each informing and enriching the other. As society's understanding of gender evolves, so too does the feminist movement, which increasingly recognizes the diverse experiences and identities of individuals. This interplay between gender identity and feminism is vital for fostering inclusivity and equality, as it challenges traditional notions of gender and advocates for the rights and recognition of all gender identities.

Gender identity refers to an individual's deeply felt experience of their own gender, which may or may not align with the sex assigned at birth. It encompasses a spectrum of identities, including but not limited to cisgender, transgender, non-binary, genderqueer, and genderfluid. Each person's gender identity is unique and can shape their experiences, perspectives, and interactions with the world.

Feminism, at its core, seeks to dismantle patriarchal structures and promote equality for all genders. Historically, the feminist movement has focused on issues of gender inequality faced by women, particularly cisgender women. However, as awareness of diverse gender identities grows, feminism has expanded to include the experiences and rights of transgender and non-binary individuals. This evolution reflects a broader commitment to intersectionality, which recognizes that gender identity intersects with other aspects of identity, such as race, class, sexuality, and ability.

For feminism to be truly inclusive, it must embrace the full spectrum of gender identities and advocate for the rights and dignity of all individuals. This involves challenging societal norms and stereotypes that dictate rigid gender roles and expectations. By questioning these norms, feminism can create space for diverse expressions of gender and empower individuals to define their own identities.

One of the ways feminism intersects with gender identity is through the advocacy for transgender rights. Transgender individuals often face significant discrimination and marginalization, both within and outside the feminist movement. Issues such as access to healthcare, legal recognition, and protection from violence and discrimination are critical areas where feminist advocacy can make a meaningful impact. By supporting policies and initiatives that promote the rights and wellbeing of transgender individuals, feminism can contribute to a more equitable and inclusive society.

Non-binary and genderqueer identities also challenge traditional feminist frameworks, which have historically been centered around a binary understanding of gender. These identities highlight the limitations of a binary system and emphasize the fluidity and diversity of gender. Feminism can embrace this complexity by adopting a more expansive and inclusive approach that acknowledges and values non-binary experiences.

Education and awareness-raising are essential components of fostering an inclusive feminist movement. By educating individuals about the diversity of gender identities and the unique challenges faced by transgender and non-binary individuals, feminism can build a more informed and empathetic base of supporters. This includes challenging misconceptions and stereotypes, promoting understanding and acceptance, and encouraging individuals to reflect on their own biases and assumptions.

Language plays a crucial role in the interplay between gender identity and feminism. Inclusive language can affirm and validate diverse gender identities, while exclusionary language can perpetuate marginalization. Feminism can lead the way in promoting language that respects and acknowledges all gender identities, such as using individuals' chosen names and pronouns and adopting gender-neutral terms where appropriate.

Collaboration and allyship are vital in advancing gender identity and feminist solidarity. By building alliances with LGBTQ+ organizations and activists, feminist movements can strengthen their impact and reach. These partnerships allow for the sharing of resources, knowledge, and strategies, enhancing the effectiveness of collective action. Allyship involves actively supporting and advocating for the rights and recognition of transgender and non-binary individuals, while also amplifying their voices and leadership within the movement.

The intersection of gender identity and feminism also calls for a reevaluation of traditional feminist goals and priorities. Issues such as reproductive rights, workplace equality, and gender-based violence must be addressed with an understanding of how they uniquely affect individuals across the gender spectrum. For example, access to reproductive healthcare must consider the needs of transgender and non-binary individuals, while efforts to combat gender-based violence must address the specific vulnerabilities faced by these communities.

Incorporating gender identity into feminist frameworks requires a commitment to ongoing reflection and adaptation. As society's understanding of gender continues to evolve, feminism must remain open to new ideas and perspectives. This includes listening to and learning from the experiences of transgender and non-binary individuals, as well as acknowledging and addressing the ways in which feminism has historically excluded or marginalized these voices.

Queer Theory and Intersectional Feminism

Queer theory and intersectional feminism converge in a rich dialogue that seeks to unravel the complexities of identity, power, and resistance. Both frameworks challenge normative structures and question the binaries that have long dominated societal understanding. By examining the interplay between these two approaches, we uncover a landscape where diverse identities and experiences are not only acknowledged but celebrated and where the fight for equality becomes a more inclusive, nuanced endeavor.

Queer theory emerged in the late 20th century as a critical response to normative understandings of sexuality and gender. It seeks to deconstruct fixed categories, such as heterosexuality and homosexuality, and instead emphasizes the fluidity and performativity of these identities. Queer theory critiques the societal structures that enforce rigid binaries and norms, advocating for a world where diverse sexualities and gender expressions are recognized and valued.

Intersectional feminism, on the other hand, emerged from the need to address the limitations of mainstream feminism, which often centered on the experiences of white, middle-class women. Coined by Kimberlé Crenshaw, intersectionality is a framework that examines how various forms of oppression, such as racism, sexism, classism, and more, intersect and compound to affect individuals' experiences. Intersectional feminism acknowledges that gender is not an isolated category of analysis but is intertwined with other aspects of identity, such as race, class, sexuality, and ability.

The convergence of queer theory and intersectional feminism offers a comprehensive approach to understanding identity and power dynamics. Both frameworks emphasize the importance of dismantling oppressive systems and recognizing the multifaceted nature of identity. By integrating these perspectives, we can develop a more inclusive and effective movement for social justice.

One of the key contributions of queer theory to intersectional feminism is its critique of normative gender and sexual identities. Queer theory challenges the idea of fixed, binary identities and highlights the fluidity and diversity of human experiences. This perspective aligns with intersectional feminism's commitment to recognizing the complexity of identities and experiences, acknowledging that individuals may simultaneously experience privilege and oppression in different contexts.

Queer theory also expands intersectional feminism's understanding of gender by emphasizing the performative aspects of identity. Drawing on the work of theorists like Judith Butler, queer theory posits that gender is not an innate characteristic but is performed through repeated actions and behaviors. This idea resonates with intersectional feminism's focus on challenging societal norms and structures, encouraging individuals to question and resist the roles and expectations imposed upon them.

In practice, the integration of queer theory and intersectional feminism can inform activism, advocacy, and policy-making. For instance, efforts to combat gender-based violence can benefit from both frameworks by acknowledging the diverse experiences of survivors and addressing the specific vulnerabilities faced by LGBTQ+ individuals, people of color, and those with disabilities. By adopting an intersectional, queer-informed approach, activists can develop more targeted and effective strategies for prevention and support.

Education is another area where the synergy between queer theory and intersectional feminism can drive meaningful change. By incorporating these frameworks into educational curricula, educators can foster critical thinking and empathy among students, encouraging them to challenge stereotypes and embrace diversity. This approach can also create more inclusive learning environments where all students feel valued and respected.

Healthcare is a critical domain where queer theory and intersectional feminism intersect. LGBTQ+ individuals, particularly those from marginalized communities, often face barriers to accessing healthcare services, including discrimination, lack of provider knowledge, and inadequate coverage for gender-affirming care. By advocating for policies and practices that prioritize inclusivity and equity, activists can work towards a healthcare system that addresses the unique needs of all individuals, regardless of their gender identity or sexual orientation.

The workplace is another area where the integration of queer theory and intersectional feminism can promote equity and inclusion. By challenging traditional norms and advocating for policies that support diverse identities, such as inclusive hiring practices, anti-discrimination policies, and support for LGBTQ+ employees, organizations can create environments where all individuals can thrive and contribute.

The arts and media also offer powerful platforms for expressing the themes of queer theory and intersectional feminism. By amplifying diverse voices and challenging dominant narratives, artists and creators can foster greater understanding and acceptance of diverse identities and experiences. This cultural representation can play a crucial role in shifting societal attitudes and promoting empathy and inclusivity.

Community-building is an essential aspect of advancing the goals of queer theory and intersectional feminism. By fostering spaces where individuals can connect, share experiences, and support one another, communities can build solidarity and resilience in the face of oppression. These spaces can also serve as incubators for activism and advocacy, allowing individuals to collaborate on strategies for effecting change.

Allyship is a vital component of the intersection of queer theory and intersectional feminism. Allies can play a significant role in advancing the goals of these movements by supporting and amplifying the voices of marginalized individuals. This involves actively listening to and learning from the experiences of others, challenging one's own biases and assumptions, and taking action to address systemic inequalities.

Transgender Experiences and Challenges

Transgender experiences and challenges span a wide spectrum, deeply influenced by societal norms, cultural contexts, and individual journeys. For many transgender individuals, navigating the world involves confronting both personal and systemic obstacles that impact their daily lives. Understanding these challenges requires a nuanced appreciation of the diverse experiences and identities within the transgender community, as well as a commitment to fostering inclusivity and support.

One of the most significant challenges faced by transgender individuals is the process of coming out and transitioning. This journey can be both empowering and fraught with difficulty, as it often involves navigating family dynamics, social relationships, and workplace environments. Many transgender people encounter resistance or rejection from family members, which can lead to feelings of isolation and disconnection. Supportive family and friends play a crucial role in providing affirmation and acceptance, which can significantly impact an individual's mental and emotional well-being.

The workplace presents its own set of challenges for transgender individuals. Despite progress in recent years, discrimination and bias remain prevalent, with many transgender people facing barriers to employment, harassment, and a lack of inclusive policies. Employers can make a significant difference by implementing anti-discrimination policies, providing diversity training, and creating supportive environments where transgender employees feel valued and respected.

Access to healthcare is another critical issue for the transgender community. Many transgender individuals encounter obstacles in obtaining gender-affirming care, including hormone therapy, surgeries, and mental health support. These barriers can be exacerbated by a lack of knowledgeable healthcare providers, financial constraints, and discriminatory insurance practices. Expanding access to comprehensive, affirming healthcare services is essential for supporting the well-being and health of transgender individuals.

Legal recognition is a fundamental aspect of transgender rights, yet many face challenges in obtaining accurate identification documents. The process of changing gender markers on official documents can be complex, costly, and inaccessible, creating obstacles in various aspects of life, from travel to employment. Advocacy for streamlined, accessible processes for legal recognition is vital to ensure that transgender individuals can live authentically and without unnecessary barriers.

Safety and violence are significant concerns for the transgender community, particularly for transgender women of color who face disproportionately high rates of violence and discrimination. Transgender individuals often encounter harassment and violence in public spaces, contributing to a pervasive sense of vulnerability. Addressing these issues requires comprehensive policy measures, community support, and increased awareness to foster safer environments for all individuals.

Education plays a pivotal role in shaping the experiences of transgender youth. Schools can be environments of acceptance and growth or sites of bullying and exclusion. Implementing inclusive curricula, providing training for educators, and establishing supportive policies can create school environments where transgender students feel safe and empowered to thrive.

Mental health is a critical aspect of the transgender experience, with many individuals facing increased rates of anxiety, depression, and suicidal ideation due to societal stigma and discrimination. Access to affirming mental health care and support networks is vital for promoting resilience and well-being. Community organizations and peer support groups can provide invaluable spaces for connection, understanding, and empowerment.

Visibility and representation are powerful tools for challenging stereotypes and promoting acceptance. Media portrayals of transgender individuals have a significant impact on societal perceptions and can either reinforce harmful stereotypes or foster empathy and understanding. Increasing authentic and diverse representations of transgender lives in media, arts, and culture is crucial for combating stigma and promoting inclusivity.

Advocacy and activism are at the heart of driving change for transgender rights. Grassroots organizations and community leaders play a vital role in raising awareness, challenging discriminatory policies, and advocating for equality. By engaging in advocacy efforts, individuals can contribute to a broader movement for social justice and support the rights and dignity of transgender individuals.

Allyship is an essential component of supporting transgender individuals and fostering inclusivity. Allies can make a difference by educating themselves about transgender issues, challenging discriminatory behaviors, and amplifying the voices of transgender individuals. Effective allyship involves active listening, empathy, and a commitment to advocating for change both personally and within one's community.

Intersectionality is a key consideration in understanding transgender experiences, as individuals' identities are shaped by the interplay of race, class, gender, sexuality, and other factors. Recognizing the diverse experiences within the transgender community allows for more inclusive and effective advocacy and support. It is essential to center the voices and leadership of marginalized individuals, particularly transgender people of color, in efforts to promote equity and justice.

Building supportive communities is vital for fostering resilience and empowerment among transgender individuals. Community spaces that celebrate diversity and provide resources, support, and connection can create environments where individuals feel valued and able to thrive. Collaboration and solidarity within and beyond the transgender community can strengthen advocacy efforts and drive meaningful change.

Education and awareness-raising are crucial for challenging misconceptions and promoting acceptance of transgender individuals. By engaging with educational initiatives, media campaigns, and community events, individuals can contribute to a broader cultural shift towards inclusivity and empathy. These efforts can help dismantle stereotypes and foster environments where transgender individuals are respected and affirmed.

Sexual Orientation and Feminist Activism

Sexual orientation and feminist activism are deeply interwoven, forming a dynamic partnership that seeks to challenge oppressive structures and advocate for equality and justice. The relationship between these two spheres is vital for understanding the complexities of identity and the multifaceted nature of discrimination and privilege. By exploring how sexual orientation intersects with feminist activism, we can better appreciate the diverse experiences within the feminist movement and create more inclusive and effective strategies for change.

Sexual orientation encompasses a range of identities, including lesbian, gay, bisexual, pansexual, asexual, and many others. Each identity represents a unique experience and perspective, contributing to the rich tapestry of human diversity. Historically, the feminist movement has been critiqued for focusing predominantly on the experiences of heterosexual women, often sidelining the voices and concerns of LGBTQ+ individuals. However, the integration of sexual orientation into feminist activism has allowed for a more comprehensive approach to addressing gender-based injustices.

Feminist activism that embraces diverse sexual orientations recognizes that the fight for gender equality must also include the fight for sexual orientation equality. This means challenging heteronormative structures that privilege heterosexual relationships and marginalize or erase LGBTQ+ experiences. By advocating for policies that protect the rights and dignity of all individuals, regardless of sexual orientation, feminist activism can contribute to a more inclusive society.

One area where sexual orientation and feminist activism intersect is in the realm of family and relationship rights. The legal recognition of same-sex marriages and partnerships has been a significant focus of activism, as it directly impacts the rights and protections afforded to LGBTQ+ individuals and families. Feminist activists have played a crucial role in advocating for marriage equality, as well as for the recognition of diverse family structures that go beyond the traditional nuclear model.

Reproductive rights and healthcare access are also critical issues at the intersection of sexual orientation and feminist activism. LGBTQ+ individuals, particularly those assigned female at birth, face unique challenges in accessing reproductive healthcare, including discrimination from providers and a lack of inclusive services. Feminist activism can address these disparities by advocating for comprehensive, affirming healthcare that meets the needs of all individuals, regardless of their sexual orientation.

Workplace equality is another domain where sexual orientation and feminist activism converge. LGBTQ+ individuals often encounter discrimination and bias in the workplace, affecting their career advancement and job security. Feminist activism can support efforts to create inclusive work environments by advocating for anti-discrimination policies, diversity training, and the recognition of diverse identities in hiring and promotion practices.

Education is a powerful tool for fostering understanding and acceptance, and feminist activism can play a vital role in promoting inclusive curricula that reflect the diversity of sexual orientations. By integrating LGBTQ+ history, literature, and perspectives into educational programs, schools can create environments where all students feel seen and valued. This educational approach not only benefits LGBTQ+ students but also enriches the learning experience for all students by promoting empathy and critical thinking.

Cultural representation is another area where sexual orientation and feminist activism intersect. Media portrayals of LGBTQ+ individuals have a significant impact on societal attitudes and can either reinforce harmful stereotypes or foster acceptance and understanding. Feminist activists can advocate for diverse and authentic representations of LGBTQ+ lives in film, television, literature, and other cultural mediums, challenging norms and promoting visibility.

Community building is a cornerstone of feminist activism, and creating supportive spaces for LGBTQ+ individuals is essential for fostering resilience and empowerment. LGBTQ+ community centers, support groups, and social networks provide vital resources and connections, allowing individuals to share experiences and advocate for change. Feminist activism can support these efforts by promoting solidarity and collaboration within and beyond LGBTQ+ communities.

Allyship is a crucial aspect of supporting LGBTQ+ individuals within feminist activism. Allies can make a significant impact by educating themselves about

LGBTQ+ issues, challenging discriminatory behaviors, and amplifying the voices of LGBTQ+ individuals. Effective allyship involves active listening, empathy, and a commitment to advocating for change both personally and within one's community.

Intersectionality is a key consideration in understanding the relationship between sexual orientation and feminist activism. Individuals' experiences are shaped by the interplay of various aspects of identity, including race, class, gender, and ability. Recognizing this complexity allows for more inclusive and effective advocacy and support. It is essential to center the voices and leadership of marginalized individuals, particularly LGBTQ+ people of color, in efforts to promote equity and justice.

Advocacy and activism are at the heart of driving change for LGBTQ+ rights, and feminist activists have played a pivotal role in challenging discriminatory policies and raising awareness. By engaging in advocacy efforts, individuals can contribute to a broader movement for social justice and support the rights and dignity of LGBTQ+ individuals.

Building Inclusive Feminist Movements

Creating feminist movements that embrace inclusivity is a transformative endeavor, essential for addressing the diverse needs of all individuals affected by gender-based discrimination. Such movements are defined not only by their goals but also by the breadth of voices they include and amplify. They seek to dismantle the hierarchical structures that have historically marginalized certain groups, making way for a more equitable and representative advocacy landscape.

A truly inclusive feminist movement begins with an understanding of intersectionality—a concept that highlights how various forms of discrimination, such as those based on race, class, sexuality, and ability, intersect and compound. By centering intersectionality, feminist movements can ensure that they address the multifaceted nature of oppression and create strategies that resonate with a broader audience. This approach requires a commitment to listening and learning from those whose voices have often been marginalized within mainstream feminism, including women of color, LGBTQ+ individuals, and those with disabilities.

Listening is a crucial component of building inclusivity. This involves creating spaces where diverse voices can share their experiences and perspectives without fear of dismissal or tokenization. Community forums, workshops, and listening sessions can provide opportunities for individuals to express their concerns and ideas, fostering a sense of belonging and empowerment. By prioritizing the voices of those most affected by inequality, feminist movements can ensure that their actions are informed by lived experiences and grounded in the realities of those they aim to support.

Amplifying marginalized voices also involves actively seeking out and supporting leadership from within these communities. Representation matters, and when individuals from diverse backgrounds lead movements, it signals a genuine commitment to inclusivity. This leadership can take many forms, from grassroots organizers to public speakers, writers, and artists. By uplifting these leaders, feminist movements can challenge traditional power dynamics and demonstrate the strength of diversity.

Education is another critical aspect of building inclusive feminist movements. Providing resources and training on intersectionality, privilege, and bias can help members of the movement understand the complexities of oppression and the importance of allyship. Workshops, reading groups, and discussions can facilitate this learning, creating a culture of ongoing reflection and growth. By fostering an environment where members are encouraged to challenge their own assumptions and engage with different perspectives, feminist movements can cultivate empathy and solidarity.

Collaboration is key to expanding the reach and impact of inclusive feminist movements. Building coalitions with other social justice organizations allows for the sharing of resources, knowledge, and strategies. These partnerships can amplify the voices of marginalized groups and create a united front against systemic oppression. By working together, movements can address interconnected issues such as economic inequality, racial justice, and environmental sustainability, recognizing that these struggles are interconnected and require collective action.

Policy advocacy is another avenue for advancing inclusivity within feminist movements. By pushing for legal and institutional changes that protect the rights of all individuals, movements can create tangible improvements in people's lives. This includes advocating for policies that address wage inequality, reproductive justice, and anti-discrimination protections, as well as those that specifically benefit marginalized communities, such as healthcare access for transgender individuals and protections for undocumented immigrants. Engaging in policy advocacy requires a strategic approach, leveraging research, storytelling, and grassroots mobilization to effect change.

Creating inclusive feminist movements also involves challenging and redefining traditional narratives of feminism. Moving away from a singular focus on gender, these movements embrace a broader understanding of identity and oppression. This means recognizing that issues like immigration, housing, and education are feminist issues, as they disproportionately affect marginalized women and gender minorities. By broadening the scope of feminist activism, movements can engage a wider audience and build stronger alliances.

Art and culture play a vital role in shaping and expressing the values of inclusive feminist movements. Through storytelling, visual art, and performance, artists can bring attention to the experiences of marginalized communities and challenge dominant narratives. Art has the power to inspire, provoke, and connect, making it a valuable tool for advocacy and education. By supporting and promoting the work of diverse artists, feminist movements can harness the power of creativity to drive social change.

Technology and social media offer new opportunities for building inclusive feminist movements. These platforms can connect individuals across geographical and cultural boundaries, facilitating the sharing of ideas and resources. Social media campaigns can raise awareness of issues and mobilize support for action, while online communities provide spaces for connection and solidarity. However, it is important to recognize the digital divide and ensure that technology is used in ways that are accessible and equitable.

Accountability is essential for maintaining the integrity and inclusivity of feminist movements. This involves being open to feedback and criticism, acknowledging mistakes, and committing to continual improvement. Establishing mechanisms for transparency and accountability, such as advisory boards or community councils, can help movements stay true to their values and ensure that they remain responsive to the needs of their members.

Chapter 5

Disability, Health, and Feminist Advocacy

Disability Rights and Feminist Thought

Disability rights and feminist thought have long intersected in ways that challenge traditional understandings of ability, autonomy, and equality. Both movements seek to dismantle societal structures that perpetuate exclusion and discrimination, striving for a more inclusive world where all individuals can thrive. By examining the connections between disability rights and feminist thought, we can gain a deeper appreciation of the diverse experiences and needs of individuals at the intersections of these identities.

The disability rights movement emerged as a response to the systemic marginalization and discrimination faced by individuals with disabilities. Advocates have fought for legal protections, access to education, employment opportunities, and the removal of physical and social barriers. The movement emphasizes the importance of autonomy, dignity, and the right to self-determination for individuals with disabilities.

Feminist thought, similarly, has long been concerned with challenging oppressive systems that limit individuals' autonomy and potential. By interrogating the ways in which gender intersects with other aspects of identity, feminist thought seeks to uncover and address the root causes of inequality. This includes examining how traditional gender roles and expectations have contributed to the marginalization of individuals with disabilities.

One key area where disability rights and feminist thought intersect is in the critique of the medical model of disability. This model views disability as a defect or deficiency that needs to be fixed or cured, often ignoring the social and environmental factors that contribute to individuals' experiences. Feminist thought challenges this perspective by emphasizing the social model of disability, which views disability as a result of societal barriers and attitudes rather than an individual's inherent limitations. By adopting the social model, both movements advocate for a shift in focus from individual impairment to societal change.

Reproductive rights and healthcare access are critical issues at the intersection of disability rights and feminist thought. Individuals with disabilities often face unique challenges in accessing comprehensive, affirming healthcare services, including reproductive care. These challenges can be exacerbated by societal assumptions about disability and sexuality, as well as a lack of healthcare providers trained to meet the needs of individuals with disabilities. Feminist thought can inform approaches to healthcare that prioritize the autonomy and dignity of all individuals, advocating for policies that ensure equitable access to services.

Education is another domain where the intersection of disability rights and feminist thought can drive meaningful change. Inclusive educational practices that accommodate diverse learning styles and abilities can create environments where all students, regardless of gender or disability, can thrive. By advocating for curricula that reflect the diverse experiences of individuals with disabilities, feminist thought can contribute to a more comprehensive and empathetic understanding of disability within educational settings.

Employment and economic justice are also critical areas of focus for both movements. Individuals with disabilities often face barriers to employment, including discrimination, lack of accommodations, and limited opportunities. Feminist thought can address these disparities by advocating for policies that promote workplace inclusivity, such as anti-discrimination legislation, accessible workplaces, and equitable pay. By challenging traditional notions of productivity and value, feminist thought can contribute to a more inclusive understanding of work and economic participation.

Cultural representation is a powerful tool for challenging stereotypes and promoting acceptance of individuals with disabilities. Media portrayals of disability can either reinforce harmful stereotypes or foster empathy and understanding. Feminist thought can advocate for diverse and authentic representations of disability in film, television, literature, and other cultural mediums, challenging norms and promoting visibility. By amplifying the voices of individuals with disabilities, cultural representation can contribute to a broader societal shift towards inclusivity.

Community building is a cornerstone of both disability rights and feminist thought, providing spaces for individuals to connect, share experiences, and advocate for change. Support networks, peer groups, and community organizations offer vital resources and connections, fostering resilience and empowerment. By promoting solidarity and collaboration within and beyond disability communities, feminist thought can contribute to stronger, more inclusive advocacy efforts.

Allyship is an essential component of supporting individuals with disabilities within feminist thought. Allies can make a significant impact by educating themselves about disability issues, challenging discriminatory behaviors, and amplifying the voices of individuals with disabilities. Effective allyship involves active listening, empathy, and a commitment to advocating for change both personally and within one's community. By recognizing and addressing the unique challenges faced by individuals with disabilities, allies can contribute to a more inclusive and equitable society.

Accessibility is a fundamental principle at the intersection of disability rights and feminist thought. Ensuring that physical and digital spaces are accessible to all individuals is essential for promoting inclusion and participation. This includes advocating for universal design principles, which prioritize accessibility from the outset, as well as for policies that address barriers to access in transportation, housing, and public spaces. By prioritizing accessibility, feminist thought can contribute to a world where all individuals can engage fully and equally in society.

Intersectionality is a key consideration in understanding the relationship between disability rights and feminist thought. Individuals' experiences are shaped by the interplay of various aspects of identity, including race, class, gender, and ability. Recognizing this complexity allows for more inclusive and effective advocacy and support. It is essential to center the voices and leadership of marginalized individuals, particularly those at the intersections of multiple identities, in efforts to promote equity and justice.

Policy advocacy is a critical avenue for advancing disability rights within feminist thought. By pushing for legal and institutional changes that protect the rights of individuals with disabilities, movements can create tangible improvements in people's lives. This includes advocating for policies that address accessibility, healthcare, education, and employment, as well as those that specifically benefit marginalized communities. Engaging in policy advocacy requires a strategic approach, leveraging research, storytelling, and grassroots mobilization to effect change.

Health Disparities and Gender Inequality

Health disparities and gender inequality are deeply intertwined, impacting the well-being and quality of life of individuals across the globe. Understanding these disparities requires a nuanced examination of the social, economic, and cultural factors that contribute to unequal health outcomes. By addressing these issues, we can work towards creating a more equitable healthcare system that serves the needs of all individuals, regardless of gender.

Gender inequality manifests in various ways within healthcare systems, influencing access to care, quality of treatment, and overall health outcomes. Women, transgender, and non-binary individuals often face unique challenges in accessing healthcare services, which can be exacerbated by intersecting factors such as race, socioeconomic status, and geographic location. These disparities are not solely the result of individual circumstances but are also perpetuated by systemic biases that prioritize certain groups over others.

One of the most significant barriers to equitable healthcare is access. Women and gender minorities frequently encounter obstacles in obtaining the care they need, whether due to financial constraints, lack of transportation, or limited availability of services. In many regions, healthcare facilities are concentrated in urban areas, making it difficult for those in rural or underserved communities to access care. Addressing these geographical disparities requires targeted investments in healthcare infrastructure and transportation services to ensure that all individuals can reach the care they need.

Economic factors also play a critical role in shaping health disparities. Women, on average, earn less than men, which can limit their ability to afford healthcare services, insurance, and necessary medications. This economic inequality is compounded by the fact that women often bear the brunt of unpaid caregiving responsibilities, further reducing their financial independence and access to healthcare. Policy interventions such as equal pay legislation, affordable childcare, and expanded healthcare coverage are essential for mitigating these economic barriers and promoting gender equality in health access.

Cultural norms and gender roles can also influence health behaviors and access to care. In some communities, traditional gender roles may discourage women from seeking medical attention or participating in preventive health measures. Additionally, stigma and discrimination against transgender and non-binary individuals can lead to delays in seeking care or avoidance of healthcare services altogether. Culturally sensitive education and outreach programs can help challenge these norms and empower individuals to take charge of their health.

Within the healthcare system itself, gender biases can affect the quality of care received by women and gender minorities. Research has shown that women are often underrepresented in clinical trials, leading to a lack of data on how treatments affect them differently than men. This gap in knowledge can result in misdiagnosis or inappropriate treatment. Furthermore, women and gender minorities may face implicit biases from healthcare providers, resulting in their symptoms being dismissed or minimized. Addressing these biases requires comprehensive training for healthcare professionals to ensure that they provide equitable and respectful care to all patients.

Reproductive health is a critical area where health disparities and gender inequality converge. Access to reproductive health services, including contraception, prenatal care, and safe abortion, is essential for women's health and autonomy. However, many individuals face barriers to accessing these services due to restrictive policies, lack of availability, or cultural stigma. Advocacy for reproductive rights and the expansion of accessible, affordable reproductive healthcare services are vital for promoting gender equality and improving health outcomes.

Mental health is another domain where gender disparities are evident. Women are more likely than men to experience certain mental health conditions, such as anxiety and depression, yet they may face barriers to accessing mental health services. Additionally, transgender and non-binary individuals often experience higher rates of mental health issues due to societal discrimination and stigma. Expanding access to mental health services and integrating mental health care into primary healthcare settings can help address these disparities and ensure that individuals receive the support they need.

The intersection of gender and other social determinants of health, such as race and socioeconomic status, further compounds health disparities. Women of color, for example, often face multiple layers of discrimination that exacerbate health inequities. These intersecting factors can result in higher rates of chronic conditions, limited access to care, and poorer health outcomes. Efforts to address health disparities must take an intersectional approach, recognizing and addressing the unique challenges faced by individuals at the intersections of multiple identities.

Public health initiatives play a crucial role in addressing health disparities and promoting gender equality. Community-based programs that focus on preventive care, education, and outreach can empower individuals to make informed health decisions and access necessary services. These programs should be designed with input from the communities they serve to ensure that they are culturally relevant and effective.

Policy advocacy is essential for driving systemic change and addressing the root causes of health disparities. This includes advocating for policies that promote gender equality, such as paid family leave, affordable childcare, and comprehensive healthcare coverage. Additionally, policies that address social determinants of health, such as housing, education, and employment, can have a significant impact on health outcomes and contribute to greater gender equity.

Research plays a vital role in understanding and addressing health disparities. By investing in research that examines the impact of gender on health outcomes, we can develop more targeted and effective interventions. This includes increasing representation in clinical trials and conducting studies that explore the unique health needs of women and gender minorities.

Community engagement is also critical for promoting health equity and gender equality. By involving individuals and communities in the design and implementation of health programs, we can ensure that interventions are responsive to the needs and priorities of those they aim to serve. Community engagement fosters trust, collaboration, and empowerment, creating a foundation for lasting change.

Reproductive Rights and Access to Care

Reproductive rights and access to care are fundamental components of gender equality and personal autonomy, influencing the lives and futures of individuals around the world. At the heart of these issues is the belief that everyone should have the freedom to make informed decisions about their reproductive health without facing discrimination, coercion, or violence. Understanding the complexities of reproductive rights involves examining the barriers that individuals face in accessing care, as well as the broader social and political contexts that shape these experiences.

Access to reproductive healthcare is a multifaceted issue, encompassing a range of services such as contraception, family planning, prenatal and postnatal care, and safe abortion. These services are essential for individuals to maintain their reproductive health and exercise control over their reproductive choices. However, access to these services is often impeded by a variety of obstacles, including legal restrictions, financial barriers, and cultural stigmas.

Legal restrictions on reproductive healthcare can significantly limit individuals' ability to access necessary services. In many regions, laws and policies restrict access to contraception and abortion, often requiring individuals to navigate complex legal and bureaucratic hurdles to obtain care. These restrictions are frequently rooted in political and ideological beliefs that prioritize certain moral or religious values over individuals' rights to autonomy and privacy. Advocacy for legal reform is crucial to ensuring that reproductive rights are protected and that individuals can access the care they need without fear of legal repercussions.

Financial barriers also play a significant role in limiting access to reproductive healthcare. The cost of services, including contraception, prenatal care, and abortion, can be prohibitive for many individuals, particularly those without health insurance or with limited financial resources. Economic inequality exacerbates these challenges, as marginalized communities often face higher rates of poverty and reduced access to affordable healthcare. Expanding healthcare coverage, reducing out-of-pocket costs, and providing financial assistance for low-income individuals are essential strategies for addressing these disparities and ensuring equitable access to care.

Cultural and societal norms can further hinder access to reproductive healthcare by perpetuating stigma and misinformation. In some communities, discussing reproductive health is taboo, leading to a lack of knowledge about available services and options. Stigma surrounding certain services, such as abortion, can also deter individuals from seeking care for fear of judgment or ostracism. Comprehensive sex education and public awareness campaigns are critical for challenging these norms and empowering individuals to make informed decisions about their reproductive health.

Healthcare infrastructure and provider availability are additional factors that impact access to reproductive care. In many areas, particularly rural or underserved regions, there may be a shortage of healthcare providers trained to offer comprehensive reproductive health services. This can result in long wait times, limited service options, and reduced quality of care. Investing in healthcare infrastructure, training providers, and expanding telehealth services can help address these challenges and improve access to care for all individuals.

Reproductive rights are inherently linked to broader issues of gender equality and social justice. Individuals' ability to make autonomous decisions about their reproductive health is influenced by their social and economic status, as well as by intersecting forms of discrimination based on race, ethnicity, sexuality, and ability. Addressing reproductive rights requires an intersectional approach that recognizes and addresses these overlapping factors, ensuring that all individuals have the opportunity to exercise their rights fully and without discrimination.

Advocacy and activism play a crucial role in advancing reproductive rights and expanding access to care. Grassroots organizations, community leaders, and activists work tirelessly to raise awareness, challenge restrictive policies, and support individuals in accessing the care they need. These efforts are bolstered by legal challenges, public demonstrations, and advocacy campaigns that aim to shift public opinion and influence policymakers. By building coalitions and fostering solidarity among diverse communities, activists can amplify their voices and drive meaningful change.

Internationally, reproductive rights are recognized as a critical component of human rights. Global initiatives and treaties, such as the United Nations' Sustainable Development Goals, emphasize the importance of ensuring universal access to reproductive healthcare as part of broader efforts to promote gender equality and improve health outcomes. International collaboration and support can provide valuable resources and expertise to local efforts, helping to strengthen reproductive rights advocacy and improve access to care worldwide.

Technology and innovation offer new opportunities for expanding access to reproductive healthcare. Digital health platforms, mobile applications, and telehealth services can provide individuals with information, support, and care regardless of their location. These tools can be particularly valuable for reaching underserved communities and overcoming barriers related to distance and provider availability. Ensuring that these technologies are accessible and equitable is essential for maximizing their impact and promoting inclusive access to care.

Education is a powerful tool for empowering individuals to make informed decisions about their reproductive health. Comprehensive sex education programs that provide accurate, age-appropriate information about reproductive health and rights can equip individuals with the knowledge they need to navigate their options and advocate for their needs. By fostering a culture of openness and understanding, education can challenge stigma and support individuals in making autonomous, informed choices about their reproductive health.

Policy change is essential for addressing systemic barriers to reproductive healthcare and ensuring that all individuals can access the services they need. This includes advocating for policies that protect reproductive rights, expand healthcare coverage, and address social determinants of health that impact access to care. Policymakers must also consider the unique needs of marginalized communities and prioritize initiatives that promote equity and inclusion in reproductive healthcare.

Community engagement and support are vital for creating environments where individuals feel empowered to exercise their reproductive rights. Community-based organizations and support networks offer valuable resources, education, and advocacy, helping individuals navigate the complexities of reproductive healthcare and access the services they need. By fostering a sense of solidarity and support, these organizations can empower individuals to advocate for their rights and contribute to broader efforts to advance reproductive justice.

Mental Health and Intersectional Feminism

Mental health and intersectional feminism intersect in profound ways, shedding light on the complex and multifaceted experiences of individuals who navigate both mental health challenges and intersecting identities. By integrating an intersectional feminist perspective, we can better understand the diverse factors that influence mental health and advocate for more inclusive, equitable support systems.

Intersectional feminism, a term popularized by scholar Kimberlé Crenshaw, recognizes that individuals' experiences are shaped by the interplay of multiple aspects of identity, such as race, gender, sexuality, socioeconomic status, and ability. This framework highlights the need to address the unique challenges faced by marginalized groups, whose experiences may be overlooked or misunderstood within traditional mental health paradigms.

Mental health is not experienced in a vacuum; it is deeply influenced by social determinants and systemic inequalities. For instance, individuals from marginalized communities often face higher rates of mental health issues due to the cumulative effects of discrimination, poverty, and limited access to resources. The stress and trauma associated with these experiences can exacerbate mental health challenges, making it essential to address the root causes of inequality in mental health care.

Stigma surrounding mental health is pervasive, and it can be particularly pronounced for individuals with intersecting marginalized identities. Cultural stereotypes, societal expectations, and discriminatory practices can all contribute to an environment where individuals feel ashamed or hesitant to seek help. An intersectional feminist approach to mental health seeks to dismantle these stigmas by promoting understanding, empathy, and acceptance.

Access to mental health care is a significant barrier for many individuals, particularly those from marginalized communities. Economic disparities, geographic limitations, and a lack of culturally competent providers can all impede access to necessary services. By advocating for policies that expand access to affordable, quality mental health care, intersectional feminism can help ensure that all individuals receive the support they need.

Culturally competent care is crucial for addressing the diverse needs of individuals with intersecting identities. Mental health providers must be equipped with the knowledge and skills to understand and respect the cultural, social, and historical contexts that shape individuals' experiences. This includes recognizing the impact of systemic oppression and trauma on mental health and providing care that is sensitive to these realities. Training and education for mental health professionals are essential for fostering a more inclusive and responsive mental health care system.

Community-based mental health initiatives can play a vital role in supporting individuals with intersecting identities. Peer support groups, community organizations, and grassroots movements offer valuable resources and connections, providing spaces where individuals can share experiences, find solidarity, and advocate for change. By centering the voices and leadership of marginalized individuals, these initiatives can create more effective and empowering mental health support systems.

Storytelling and narrative therapy are powerful tools for healing and empowerment within an intersectional feminist framework. By sharing personal stories and experiences, individuals can challenge dominant narratives and reclaim agency over their mental health journeys. This process of storytelling can also foster empathy and understanding, helping to bridge gaps between diverse communities and promote collective healing.

Advocacy and activism are integral to advancing mental health equity within an intersectional feminist context. By raising awareness, challenging oppressive systems, and advocating for policy change, activists can drive meaningful improvements in mental health care access and quality. Collaborative efforts that bring together diverse voices and perspectives are essential for building a more inclusive mental health care system that serves all individuals.

Education and outreach are critical components of promoting mental health awareness and reducing stigma. Comprehensive mental health education programs can equip individuals with the knowledge and skills to recognize and address mental health challenges, both in themselves and in others. These programs should be inclusive and culturally relevant, addressing the unique needs and experiences of individuals with intersecting identities.

Policy change is essential for addressing systemic barriers to mental health care and ensuring that all individuals can access the services they need. This includes advocating for policies that promote mental health parity, expand healthcare coverage, and address social determinants of health. Policymakers must also consider the unique needs of marginalized communities and prioritize initiatives that promote equity and inclusion in mental health care.

Research plays a vital role in understanding and addressing mental health disparities. By investing in research that examines the impact of intersectionality on mental health outcomes, we can develop more targeted and effective interventions. This includes increasing representation in mental health research and conducting studies that explore the unique mental health needs of individuals with intersecting identities.

Technology and innovation offer new opportunities for expanding access to mental health care and support. Digital platforms, mobile applications, and telehealth services can provide individuals with information, resources, and care regardless of their location. These tools can be particularly valuable for reaching underserved communities and overcoming barriers related to distance and provider availability. Ensuring that these technologies are accessible and equitable is essential for maximizing their impact and promoting inclusive mental health care.

Empowerment and self-care are important aspects of mental health within an intersectional feminist framework. Encouraging individuals to prioritize their mental well-being and engage in self-care practices can help build resilience and support overall mental health. This includes promoting mindfulness, stress reduction, and coping strategies that are culturally relevant and accessible to individuals with diverse identities and experiences.

Collaboration and solidarity are key to building a more inclusive and equitable mental health care system. By fostering partnerships between mental health professionals, community organizations, and individuals with lived experience, we can create more effective support networks and drive systemic change. These collaborative efforts should prioritize the voices and leadership of marginalized individuals and communities, recognizing their expertise and contributions to mental health advocacy.

Case Studies Disabled Women in Activism

The story of disabled women in activism is a testament to resilience, courage, and the relentless pursuit of justice. Their efforts have not only highlighted the unique challenges faced by disabled individuals but have also paved the way for more inclusive social movements. These women have defied societal expectations, using their voices and experiences to drive meaningful change and inspire future generations. Through their advocacy, they have redefined what it means to be an activist, challenging the notion that disability is a limitation rather than a source of strength.

Consider Judy Heumann, a pioneering figure in the disability rights movement. Born in Brooklyn in 1947, Heumann contracted polio at just 18 months old, leaving her reliant on a wheelchair for mobility. Faced with discrimination from a young age, she was denied the right to attend her local school due to her disability. This experience ignited a passion for advocacy that would shape her life's work. Heumann's activism was instrumental in the passage of landmark legislation, such as the Americans with Disabilities Act (ADA) and the Rehabilitation Act of 1973. Her leadership in organizing the 504 Sit-in, a protest demanding the implementation of disability rights regulations, demonstrated the power of disabled voices in effecting change. Heumann's story exemplifies the impact of intersectional activism, as she worked tirelessly to address the overlapping issues of disability, gender, and race.

Another remarkable activist, Vilissa Thompson, has been a prominent voice in advocating for disabled women of color. As a social worker and founder of Ramp Your Voice!, Thompson has dedicated her career to amplifying marginalized voices within the disability community. Her advocacy focuses on the intersectionality of race, gender, and disability, challenging the systemic barriers that often exclude disabled women of color from mainstream discourse. Through her writing and public speaking, Thompson has shed light on the unique challenges faced by this demographic, emphasizing the importance of visibility and representation in advocacy efforts. Her work has inspired a new generation of activists to embrace their identities and demand change.

Then there is the story of Alice Wong, a disabled activist and founder of the Disability Visibility Project. Wong's work emphasizes the power of storytelling in advocacy, creating spaces for disabled individuals to share their experiences and perspectives. As an Asian American woman with spinal muscular atrophy, Wong has navigated multiple layers of marginalization, using her platform to challenge stereotypes and promote inclusivity. Her project has fostered a vibrant community of disabled voices, highlighting the diversity and richness of the disability experience. Wong's advocacy demonstrates the importance of centering disabled narratives in social justice movements, reminding us that every story matters.

In the United Kingdom, Baroness Jane Campbell has been a formidable force in disability activism. Born with spinal muscular atrophy, Campbell has dedicated her life to advancing disability rights and challenging societal perceptions of disability. Her work in the House of Lords has been instrumental in shaping policies that promote accessibility and equality, reflecting her commitment to creating a more inclusive society. Campbell's activism underscores the necessity of representation in political spaces, as she advocates for the rights of disabled individuals at the highest levels of government. Her story serves as a reminder that disabled women have the power to influence policy and drive systemic change.

The narrative of disabled women in activism is incomplete without acknowledging the contributions of young activists like Greta Thunberg. Diagnosed with Asperger syndrome, Thunberg has reframed her disability as a source of strength in her fight against climate change. Her activism highlights the intersection of environmental and disability justice, as she advocates for a more sustainable future that considers the needs of all individuals. Thunberg's ability to mobilize global support for climate action demonstrates the impact of young voices in advocacy, challenging us to reconsider the potential of disabled individuals in social movements.

These stories illustrate the diverse ways in which disabled women have engaged in activism, each bringing their unique perspectives and experiences to the forefront of social change. Their work highlights the importance of intersectionality in advocacy, as they navigate the complexities of identity and challenge systemic barriers. By centering disabled voices in social justice movements, these activists remind us that true equality requires the inclusion of all individuals, regardless of ability.

The efforts of disabled women in activism have not been without challenges. They have faced societal attitudes that often dismiss or undermine their contributions, as well as physical and logistical barriers that complicate their work. Yet, these obstacles have only strengthened their resolve, driving them to find innovative solutions and build networks of support. Through collaboration and solidarity, disabled women have created spaces where their voices are heard, respected, and valued.

One such example is the #CripTheVote campaign, co-founded by Alice Wong, Gregg Beratan, and Andrew Pulrang. This movement aims to engage disabled individuals in political advocacy, emphasizing the importance of civic participation and representation. By leveraging social media and digital platforms, #CripTheVote has created an inclusive space for disabled voices in political discourse, highlighting the power of technology in modern activism. The campaign serves as a testament to the adaptability and resilience of disabled activists, as they navigate new frontiers in advocacy.

The legacy of disabled women in activism extends beyond their individual achievements, as they have laid the groundwork for future generations to continue the fight for equality. Their stories inspire us to recognize the potential of disabled individuals as leaders, advocates, and change-makers. By challenging societal norms and advocating for systemic change, these women have redefined what it means to be an activist, demonstrating that disability is not a barrier to leadership but a unique source of insight and strength.

As we reflect on the contributions of disabled women in activism, it is essential to continue supporting their efforts and amplifying their voices. This requires recognizing the intersectionality of their experiences and addressing the systemic barriers that persist in society. By fostering an environment that values diversity and inclusivity, we can create a world where all individuals have the opportunity to thrive and contribute to social change.